GAIETY OF SPIRIT

GAIETY OF SPIRIT

The Sherpas of Everest

FRANCES KLATZEL

RMB
Victoria Vancouver Calgary

Rocky Mountain Books
www.rmbooks.com

Library and Archives Canada Cataloguing in Publication

Klatzel, Frances
Gaiety of spirit : the sherpas of Everest / Frances Klatzel.

Includes bibliographical references.
ISBN 978-1-897522-98-1

1. Sherpa (Nepalese people). I. Title. II. Title: Sherpas of Everest.

DS493.9.S5K53 2010   954.96   C2010-902803-1

Printed in Canada

Rocky Mountain Books acknowledges the financial support for its publishing program from the Government
of Canada through the Canada Book Fund (CBF), Canada Council for the Arts, and the province of British
Columbia through the British Columbia Arts Council and the Book Publishing Tax Credit.

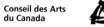

This book was produced using FSC-certified, acid-free paper,
processed chlorine free and printed with vegetable-based inks.

CONTENTS

ACKNOWLEDGEMENTS 11

PROLOGUE 15

PART ONE

MORE THAN MOUNTAINEERS, MORE THAN A MUSEUM

Gaiety of Spirit: A People Called Sherpa 19

Museum in the Clouds 27

Hearts and Minds: The Inside Culture 35

PART TWO

THE METAPHYSICAL AND THE EVERYDAY

To Perfect Our Minds 45

Places of Power 53

Beyul: The Sacred Valley 64

The Gods within You 71

PART THREE

RHYTHMS OF THE YEAR

Everyday Life 75

"Eat Potatoes, Dig Potatoes" 79

Trade and Markets 85

High Green Valleys: Summer in Khumbu 91

Winter Pilgrimage 99

PART FOUR

CEREMONY AND CELEBRATION

A Celebration of Community Spirit   105

"For the Good of the Whole World"   119

Dance of the Gods   125

PART FIVE

THE WHEEL OF LIFE

Funerals … Passages   135

Birth … Rebirth   143

The Wedding   148

PART SIX

EPILOGUE

Prayer Flags over Tin Roofs   155

Return to the Beyul   160

GLOSSARY   169

MAP OF KHUMBU VALLEY   172

SELECTED READING   173

The five colours of prayer flags signify the elements: earth, wood, water, fire and metal.

ACKNOWLEDGEMENTS

As with any project that spans several years, this book became a labour of love to which many friends and family have generously given encouragement and support.

My parents, Virginia and Stephen, first shared their love of the mountains with me, and my father's lessons in photography enabled me to continue taking photographs when the cold had killed my camera batteries and new ones were a ten-day walk away.

The late Mingma Norbu Sherpa encouraged me to write and complete this book since the idea first came at the opening of the Sherpa Cultural Centre. I am thankful for his initiative that led me to first help in Khumbu at Sagarmatha National Park and then at Tengboche. For some of the years at Tengboche, the American Himalayan Foundation generously provided a small grant for my expenses.

I will always be grateful to Tengboche Rinpoche for the opportunity to work with him on the Sherpa Cultural Centre for several years. While compiling information, our conversations often digressed to aspects of philosophy, psychology and spirituality that unveiled other ways of see-ing the world. This opportunity enriched my life, for which I will always be grateful. Many other Sherpas, such as the late Khonjo Chombi, provided invaluable cultural information during the years at Tengboche.

I would like to thank the Alberta Literary Arts Foundation for providing the grant that allowed me to write the first draft in 1994. Bob Sandford offered many years of encouragement and supported an exhibition of the photographs in Canada. Anthropologist Bruce Morrison avidly encouraged me for many years and introduced me to a literary agent, the late Joanne Kellock, who never found a publisher but taught me much about writing.

Several friends gave their time to read early drafts, and Baiba and Pat Morrow provided endless advice and assistance with photography questions. My sister and brother-in-law, Louise and Phil, and their daughters helped in many ways storing, protecting and scanning original slides.

Dr. Lhakpa Norbu Sherpa reviewed the final manuscript with commitment and attention to detail to make many valuable suggestions.* Sherap Jangbu Sherpa clarified many details and offered endless encouragement. Although every effort has been made to verify and correct the many details, any errors are my responsibility.

Many friends read various drafts of chapters over the years. Raj Khadka and Sareena Rai did edits on an early draft. In the final months of revising, I would especially like to thank Karen Barkley, Karen McDiarmid, Roger Vernon, Tim Linkins, Diki Ongmo, Shane Powers, Katelyn Mudry, the Morrows, Bart Robinson, Ben Ayers, Geoff Powter, Jane Lewkonia, Chrissie Gregory, Jocey Ansong, Ellen Coon, Doma Chudon, Wally Berg, Liesl Messerschmidt, Anne and Brian Peniston and several other friends for constructive comments, critiques and suggestions.

For the Nepal edition, I would like to thank Gael Robertson for her faith in Mera Publications, Anne Ryall for proofreading; Sonam Tashi Sherpa and all the staff of Mera Publications; and Digiscan Prepress for fine-tuning the design of the book and inserting endless corrections.

For this Canadian edition, I would like to thank Don Gorman, Chyla Cardinal and all the staff of Rocky Mountain Books for their enthusiasm for the book and patience with an author half a world away in the monsoon clouds of the Himalaya as they prepared to go to press.

Most importantly, I must express my heartfelt gratitude to the many Sherpa friends who shared their stories, thoughts and beliefs with me. Their photographs and stories are the content of this book. A few personas in the book are an invented composite of various individuals to protect their privacy and create a unified story. Other individuals kindly allowed me to use their names, photographs and stories.

I would especially like to say a big *tuche* (thank you) to Ang Dooli and family; Sherap Jangbu, Lhakpa Dolma, Rita Dolma, Mingma Gelgen and Phurba Yangjin; Ang Rita, Ang Zangmu and family; Pasang Thondup and family; Phurba Sonam and family; Ang Temba and Yangjin; Kami Tsering and family; Thubten Yeshi; Kusang Tsering; Tenzing Norbu; Phu Thundup and Lhakpa Ngutup; Pertemba; Mingma Yangji; Namdu and family; Dawa Stephen and family; Chombi and Karma; Angjie; Samje and Tsetem; Gaga Namdu, Cheme and family; Tashi Jangbu; Dawa Phuti; Phinjo; Lhakpa, Helen and family; Dr. Kami and the staff at Khunde hospital; the monks of Tengboche, the nuns of Devuche and so many other Sherpa friends. *Thulo Kanchi* will never forget your gaiety of spirit.

Frances Klatzel

July 2010

* Note: At the request of the Sherpa readers, I have used Sherpa, rather than Nepali, names and words. Hence, I have used Nauche instead of Namche, gonda instead of gompa, etc. The transliteration of Sherpa words was done according to *Through a Sherpa Window*, by Dr. Lhakpa Norbu Sherpa, 2008. The text is in Canadian English.

Ama Dablam mountain from north at Orsho

Conversations encompassed the metaphysical and the everyday.

PROLOGUE

For a moment, I wondered where to step. The mountain trail was slippery with snow, ice and mud. Cliffs rose above us. Below, steep grassy slopes fell into the canyon.

At a notch in the ridge, each Sherpa companion murmured a prayer and placed a small stone from the path on the *labtsa*, the cairn with prayer flags. I followed suit, relieved that our trekking group had safely travelled this path.

Farther along, we paused as wind and dust blasted across the pastures. We turned our backs to the wind and hid our faces in our jackets.

Seeing only the ground before me, a premonition — an impact on the back of my head and a sudden sense of nothingness. I reacted by taking two steps forward. In that instant a thick plank, blown off a nearby hut, hit the back of my ankle. Stunned, I realized that had I not moved, the plank would have struck my head.

This event was my first real experience with the Sherpa perception of place, of the power of these mountains where the metaphysical seems to merge with the everyday.

Mountain scenery had first attracted me to the Himalaya, but the warm, friendly Sherpa became my enduring connection. From 1983 to 1989 I had the opportunity and privilege to live and work with Sherpa people in the Khumbu valley of east Nepal, near Mount Everest, helping to create a museum of Sherpa culture at Tengboche monastery.

The Sherpas are renowned through the literature of adventure, usually about climbing exploits on Mount Everest. They have earned an international reputation for their work as high-altitude porters and guides on mountaineering expeditions. However, this reputation focuses on one occupation, rather than on the Sherpas' rich cultural heritage.

The museum was mostly about what the Abbot of Tengboche calls the Sherpas' "inner culture" and the importance of ceremonies that link their spiritual and physical lives. The preparation of the museum took time because it was essential to first know the people and the many dimensions of their culture in order to accurately and concisely depict it.

While compiling information for the museum, I often found that conversations encompassed aspects of philosophy, psychology and spirituality. Often the subjects we discussed wandered to the questions we seek to answer with religion or science: How did the earth begin? What happens after death? What is our relationship to nature? To our symbols in the environment?

Over the years, my questions turned from the intellectual to the intuitive. I began to experience the culture rather than question it.

Life with the Sherpas revealed different ways of seeing the world. It peeled away my preconceived notions so that I began to appreciate the significance of rituals, traditions and symbols. In the process, I was changed.

Sherpa friends introduced me to a new way of seeing the world through everyday life. Whether monk or shepherd, they know who they are and what they believe as "Sherpa people." I saw an acceptance of mystery and of questions we just cannot answer.

Living in another culture forced me to think about how it works, to confront the ironies and inconsistencies of a different way of being. Soon I realized that one layer of meaning reveals more queries within. The more one starts to understand, the more one realizes all there is to question and explore.

Looking at other cultures as different from our own, we split the whole into parts. We analyze what we see happening and ask why. For people of the other culture, it is their way of life. We examine the oddity of different traditions and customs rather than the inner purposes that might bring us into an understanding of the culture. We end up looking at how the "other" culture is different from our culture rather than at our commonness in the wholeness of humankind.

Dumchi festival in Junbesi, Solu valley, 1983

While working on the museum, I started to see and question the ironies of my own culture and gained a new way of looking at myself and at my own way of life. I was moved by what I saw and experienced. I became a believer in the value of inner culture that manifests itself in everything we do — in small actions in everyday life, in our interactions with everyone we meet and in what we think and say.

I have come to see that while outside cultures divide us, inner cultures, the core of all religions and beliefs, can bring us together.

Sherpa women sometimes work trekking.

Part One

MORE THAN MOUNTAINEERS, MORE THAN A MUSEUM

GAIETY OF SPIRIT: A PEOPLE CALLED SHERPA

April 1988. The trail winds among boulders and gnarled rhododendron trees over a low rise. The mist opens, revealing gently sloping fields and stone houses. The spire of a Buddhist stupa mimics the pointed mountain behind.

In the maze of rock walls and fields, I stop at one of the two-storey, whitewashed houses and announce my arrival in the usual Sherpa way, calling my friend's name, "Ang Dooli! Oh, Ang Dooli!"

Her head appears at an upstairs window. "Come in."

Creeping through the dark stable, I reach steep steps to the upper storey, where I emerge into the main room of Ang Dooli's home. Wooden shelves along two walls hold copper pots, striped yak-hair blankets and metal trunks. Sunbeams streaming through the windows light up the large room.

Ang Dooli is in the kitchen vigorously pumping a narrow churn to prepare the traditional Sherpa tea with butter and salt.

Ang Dooli in her kitchen

"Sit down," she commands. Colourful wool rugs cover benches around the room. This is a comfortable home.

"Have you been back in Khumbu [the Everest area] long?" she asks.

"I flew from Kathmandu to Lukla two days ago and walked to Nauche yesterday. Today I must arrive at Tengboche because porters are carrying the display panels there. We have only a month to finish the museum."

"You have worked on that museum for over five years." Ang Dooli checks the tea.

I smile. At first I had thought the museum would take two years to finish. Eventually it took much more time to learn about the Sherpa culture before the museum could be established. Creating a museum for a monastery near Mount Everest differed vastly from scheduling a project at a national park in Canada.

"You see, I had to gather information for the museum. Rinpoche [the abbot of the Tengboche monastery] insisted that this museum tell the story from the Sherpa point of view, because he is disturbed that so many foreign books present misunderstandings about the Sherpa culture."

"Yes, many foreigners think we are porters," Ang Dooli remarks, passing a glass of tea. "These foreigners," she continues, "think we are just any locals hired to carry their baggage on these rocky trails."

She is right. Most foreigners think the name "Sherpa" refers to porters or trekking guides. In reality, the Sherpas are an ethnic group — a people called Sherpa.

Porters hired at the airstrip in Lukla are carrying my own baggage — large packages of museum display panels — up the rocky trail to Tengboche. The porters represent a small cross-section of Nepal's many distinct ethnic groups.

Each group, such as the Sherpas, has its own language, culture and history. The visitors often do not realize that the people carrying their baggage may not be conversing in a common mother tongue.

Ang Dooli and I speak in Nepali, the national language that allows these diverse groups to communicate. Neither of us is speaking our mother tongue. In the eight years since I first met Ang Dooli, we have shifted from speaking in choppy English to mostly Nepali with phrases of the Sherpa language.

Traditional Sherpa jewellery.

The diverse ethnic groups of Nepal reflect the landscape of this tiny country, which is only 880 kilometres (550 miles) long. India and Tibet (China) squeeze Nepal along the southern slope of the Himalaya. Within 160 kilometres (100 miles), the land rises from tropical jungles to glaciated mountain peaks.

The first Sherpas I met gave me a sense of their place and their isolation when we crossed on the path at the start of the five-day trek into the Everest area. They were headed in the opposite direction, toward Kathmandu, and greeted me with a friendly "Good morning." I asked where they were going. "Nepal," they said to my surprise. Later, I learned that many older Sherpas and other people living beyond the rim of Kathmandu Valley still refer to the valley as "Nepal." For these Sherpas, their homeland in the mountain valleys of Solu-Khumbu was a place distinctly different.

Sherpa villages perch amid canyons and peaks in the remote valleys around Mount Everest at 2100 to 4600 metres (7,000 to 15,000 feet) above sea level. Among the highest mountain dwellers in the world, Sherpas living in the Khumbu valley number about 3,000. Another 30,000 Sherpa people live in other high valleys of eastern Nepal.

The Sherpas originated as several families who migrated from eastern Tibet and settled these uninhabited valleys about 500 years ago. Their name, *Sher-pa*, reflects those origins: "east-people." This hardy group of perhaps fifty individuals brought with them the rich traditions, religion and literature of Tibetan Buddhism.

Sunset on Nuptse, the "west peak" of Everest.

Khunde village

The Sherpa homeland is on the fringe of the uninhabitable, where soil meets rock, and rock and snow pierce the sky.

Sherpa country links the accessible and the inaccessible. The Sherpas had considered the rock walls and ice faces of the mountain peaks to be the sacrosanct domains of the gods until the first Western mountaineers arrived in Khumbu in the 1950s.

In Ang Dooli's home, photographs of one of the most famous mountaineers, Sir Edmund Hillary, and her husband, Mingma Tsering, cover the walls. Mingma works as the sirdar, the foreman, for Sir Edmund's Himalayan Trust.

Ang Dooli had shown me Mingma's "Tiger of the Snows" award medal and certificate. The British Alpine Club had presented this award to Sherpas who displayed extraordinary courage and dedication on climbing expeditions. Mingma was on the 1953 expedition when Hillary and Sherpa Tenzing Norgay made the first successful ascent of Everest. Soon after, expeditions came every year and the Sherpas became known internationally for mountaineering work.

The Sherpas' involvement in expeditions had begun four decades earlier. Although Nepal was closed to foreigners until the early 1950s, Sherpas had migrated for employment to British-ruled Darjeeling for several decades previously. Sherpa men first worked as high-altitude porters on attempts to scale the great peaks in 1907 and have participated in almost every Himalayan mountaineering expedition since.

Mountaineers praise the Sherpas' friendliness, skill, courage, loyalty and dependability. Eric Shipton, the British mountaineer and explorer of the Himalaya in the 1930s–1950s, wrote of the Sherpas:

Young student monks

Devout monk and acrobat

"It is the temperament and character of the Sherpas that have justified their renown and won them such a large place in the hearts of the Western travellers and explorers. Their most enduring characteristic is their extraordinary gaiety of spirit. More than any other people I know, they have the gift of laughter."

Ang Dooli's gaiety of spirit had helped me overcome my fear of this unknown culture. The Sherpas' laughter, generosity and hospitality had helped me see beyond their reputation.

As I finish the tea, Ang Dooli tries to fill the glass yet again, but I put it out of her reach. After a brief, intense "hospitality skirmish," I manage to put the empty glass in her dish basin. Scrambling down the ladder, I call, "*Thuche, thuche* [thank you]."

"Hey, no need to say thuche," she shouts back, the traditional Sherpa response.

Stupa at Tengboche; Tamserku peak behind

MUSEUM IN THE CLOUDS

The heavy wooden door creaks open on to a small verandah encircled with potted orange marigolds. Inside a small house, the Rinpoche of Tengboche sits cross-legged on a wide bench at one end of a room full of photographs and books.

Wrapped in a heavy maroon robe, Rinpoche gestures for me to take a seat next to an elderly Sherpa man on a bench beneath large windows.

Rinpoche is the Abbot of Tengboche monastery in the Khumbu valley. The Sherpas regard him as the reincarnate of the monastery's founder. Everyone calls him by his title, *Tengboche Rinpoche*, and rarely by his given name, Ngawang Tenzing Zangbu. Tibetan Buddhists reserve the title *Rinpoche* for special teachers and their reincarnates. The Buddhist people of the Himalaya revere thousands of rinpoches in Nepal, Tibet, Bhutan and India.

Rinpoche realized there were many misinterpretations and misunderstandings about Sherpa culture. To promote understanding of the culture, he has built a museum to first inform foreign visitors. However, his more crucial audience is young Sherpas, who will see visitors taking an "interest in our culture and then take pride in our heritage."

My work is to interpret his discussions to offer explanations of Sherpa culture to which people can relate. The work involves researching the information, taking photographs, planning the displays, coordinating translations of texts into Nepali or Tibetan, fabricating the displays and then putting it all together in the museum building.

Rinpoche's guest is a village elder, Khonjo Chombi, who is renowned for his knowledge of old Sherpa stories, songs and traditions. Sherpas acknowledge him as a guardian of their culture.

"Please, show Khonjo Chombi through the museum," he requests.

Khonjo Chombi has provided much of the information and inspiration for the museum's display texts. He has also advised most foreign researchers of the Sherpas, the first and best known

Tengboche Rinpoche

The late Khonjo Chombi Sherpa in 1985

of whom was the anthropologist Christoph von Fürer-Haimendorf, who first came to Khumbu in the mid-1950s.

Inside the museum, Khonjo Chombi inspects the historical photographs Haimendorf donated. He names each person in the photographs. "Here is Ngawang Dorje, Thakto Kalden, Passang Rinchen; they have all passed away. There I am thirty years ago; Haimendorf took that photo. There I am last year; you took that photo." He smiles.

The panel text introducing the Sherpas has generated controversy. It reads: "The Sherpas started migrating from Tibet to these secluded valleys 600 years ago." A couple of foreign anthropologists insist that the Sherpas' entry into Khumbu from Tibet was about 450 years ago and that 600 years ago is wrong.

Rinpoche and Khonjo Chombi say these modern interpretations do not consider the first Sherpa, Phachhen, who discovered Khumbu 600 years ago. We used the 600-year date, since the purpose of the museum is to tell the Sherpas' story from their own point of view.

A mural in Tibetan script outlining the Sherpa clans covers the end wall of the museum. The position of each name shows when the clan either arrived from Tibet or separated from a larger group. Khonjo Chombi points out his clan name, *Thakdopa*.

Cultural Centre and Tengboche Monastery

The father's lineage determines one's clan membership. Four main clans originally came from Kham, in eastern Tibet, to Solu-Khumbu. Each clan gave rise to several brother clans. Continuous migration has brought many new clans into the area.

Other displays describe traditional clothing, household goods, jewellery and crafts using looms and spindles. One panel shows monks printing prayer flags on a wooden block and a stone carver chiselling a prayer stone.

Khonjo Chombi asks, "You have a photo of Au'Kinzum chipping away to make *mani* stones. Why isn't there a photo of old Phurwa carving a wood block?"

Au'Kinzum, carver of prayers into stone

"For three years I tried to persuade Phurwa to let me photograph him working, but he would not even describe how he makes the blocks. So all that we have is photographs of monks printing prayer flags on the blocks.

"Last month, Phurwa was at Tengboche doing carpentry work while we were setting up the museum. He visited the museum every day to see the new displays. The day this display with the stone carver went up, Phurwa asked why I had not photographed him carving the wood blocks. I told him how I'd tried many times. The next day he brought that huge old wooden tea cup as a gift for the museum."

Khonjo Chombi laughs and then grows serious. "No matter how much you explained, it was hard for many people to imagine what the 'museum' would be. This is the first museum old Phurwa has ever seen. But we have a bigger problem. These craftsmen's sons have not learned to carve wooden blocks or mani stones. When these men are gone, no one in Khumbu will be able to make these religious things."

"Can only sons learn these crafts?"

"No, anyone could learn their crafts; but before, we followed our father's occupation. I learned trading and politics from my father. My sons run a trekking business. Our occupations are changing, but I hope someone will keep making wood blocks and mani stones."

The second floor has displays about Sherpa religion. Balancing the many levels of explanation was a challenge when writing the display texts. Spirituality, metaphysics and pragmatism all have a place in layers of meanings in the Sherpas' practice of *Mahayana* Buddhism.

On the display about Tengboche monastery, Khonjo Chombi inspects photographs of Rinpoche through the years, beginning as a teenager when the first Westerners explored the southern approach to Everest. Other photographs show him in present-day activities. He remarks, "Rinpoche has worked hard to uphold our traditions."

Khonjo Chombi examines a mannequin dressed as a traditional village lama. "Some lamas are married and some are celibate *thawas* [monks]. Not all monks are lamas. The married lama in this photo has a family. He studied with his father and other teachers so that he can perform the village ceremonies."

He sees a bone trumpet, a *kagling,* in the mannequin's hand. I explain, "We did not have an old kagling, only a new copper one. Two weeks ago a monk returned from the post office in Nauche with a battered envelope. The address was to 'Tengboche Monastery, near Mount Everest, Nepal.' There was no letter or return address but the stamp was from Germany. Inside was this old-style kagling made of bone. We'll never know where it came from, but it came just in time for the museum opening."

Khonjo Chombi in completed museum

Khonjo Chombi continues around the museum. Suddenly he starts singing an old Sherpa folk song and dancing. Soon an audience of monks and foreign trekkers surrounds Khonjo Chombi. As we applaud, he smiles. His songs and dance become the museum's real opening celebration.

Small clay Buddha statue found in temple ruins in 1989

Hearts and Minds:
The Inside Culture

April 1989. Rinpoche inspects piles of stones, broken walls and half-melted tin roofing of the burned *gonda* (gompa temple) at Tengboche monastery. Flames devoured the gonda's fifty-year-old wooden interior on the freezing night of January 19. Now, instead of the gonda's wide, sweeping roof, only broken stone walls remain.

Workers have gathered baskets of broken statues and icons from the rubble. On a flat rock, as if on an altar in the ruins, sits a tiny clay Buddha statue found in the rubble. The fire released these small statues and icons from a larger, hollow sculpture. The flames destroyed the wooden bones of the temple, but the heart remains — this little Buddha in the ruins.

When I ask how he feels about the destruction of the temple, Rinpoche responds, "The gonda is like a person — after death the spirit goes on. The spirit of our monastery persists."

Tengboche holds a special place in the hearts and minds of both Sherpas and world visitors. On a ridge in the heart of the Khumbu valley, it has become more than just a monastery. The scene of the monastery, surrounded by snow-clad peaks, realizes many people's notions of Shangri-La, of a sacred place beyond our daily existence.

Despite Tengboche's fame, the Sherpas only founded celibate monasteries relatively recently. For centuries, they practised their faith in hermitages, and each village's gonda was under the direction of married lamas who performed the rituals required by the community. A second-generation lama born in Khumbu, Buddha Tsenchen, had three sons who all taught religion, organized their communities and founded gondas in the villages. Ralpa Dorje started the gonda in Thame; Khyenpa Dorje, in Rimijung, in the gorge below Khumbu; and Sangwa Dorje, in Pangboche. The brothers started several ceremonies of the Sherpas about 380 years ago.

Top: Tengboche Monastery in 1986. Bottom: Ruins of Tengboche after fire in 1989

Lama Sangwa Dorje.

They studied first with their father and later with teachers in the mountains of Nepal and Tibet. After practising meditation retreats in remote caves, the brothers are believed to have achieved such spiritual powers that they could perform supernatural feats.

Lama Sangwa Dorje often left a record of these feats as marks in stone. Two of these stones are at Tengboche and survived the fire. They had been at one end of the dark, narrow porch along the front of the old gonda. This was the first time I could see them in natural light. One stone bore a finely etched, inch-deep handprint with spread fingers. The second, larger stone had a deep groove running down its centre.

"As Lama Sangwa Dorje sat meditating on that stone, his foot slipped and creased the rock," says Rinpoche. "I kept faith in his prediction that someday there would be a very good monastery here."

Statues holding relics of the founders of Tengboche had sat in a beautiful room on the second floor of the gonda. Only one statue, of Lama Gulu, survived the fire.

In 1914 the Abbot of Rongbuk monastery on the north side of Everest in Tibet told a devout Sherpa, Lama Gulu, to establish a celibate monastery in the Khumbu. Lama Gulu was overwhelmed at these instructions, but the Abbot consoled him by revealing their relationship as father and son in previous lifetimes.

Lama Gulu went home to Khumbu and discussed the request with other Sherpas. They proposed several sites, including a remote ridge called Tengboche. Lama Gulu returned for advice to Rongbuk, where the abbot replied, "At Tengboche, at the edge of the flat area."

Sherpas from many villages worked for three years to build a gonda for Tengboche monastery. It was completed in 1919 and the Abbot of Rongbuk came for the opening celebrations. His presence attracted Sherpas from several days' walk away. Thus Tengboche became a focal point for Sherpa religious activities and the larger community of Khumbu.

In 1932 an earthquake destroyed the monastery's gonda. Lama Gulu was not injured but passed away that night. The monks of Tengboche went to Tibet to visit the Rongbuk Abbot, who told them to rebuild the gonda. He donated some money to start the reconstruction.

Six years later a young child from Nauche was brought to the Rongbuk Abbot, who recognized him as the reincarnation of Lama Gulu. That child grew up to be Tengboche Rinpoche.

In 1988 a small hydroelectric power plant was installed at Tengboche, but the monastery's residents perhaps never understood the dangers of electricity. Whatever the cause, fire destroyed the gonda of the monastery in January 1989.

Two people risked their lives to save precious items from the burning gonda. One is a monk, Thupkay, who is custodian of the ground-floor gonda room; the other, Norbu, is a trekking guide.

Norbu says, "It was a very cold night. The new electrical system went on and off about three times. After dinner, I saw huge flames in the monastery office beside the gonda. I ran toward the gonda, but halfway, saw the wind blow the flames into the woodwork on its roof. The gonda started burning from the top down. Thupkay and I found an old expedition ladder to climb up to the second floor. We put small statues into a basket and lowered it out the window. I straddled my legs through the window to hold the ladder up to the wall."

Thupkay continues, "I carried a large statue across the room to Norbu, who lowered it down through the window on a rope. The next morning, I tried to move the statue, but it was so heavy that three of us had to lift it. We managed to save all the *thankas* [cloth scroll paintings] and half the statues and books. We could not save the paintings on the wooden wall panelling. Inside the gonda, the fire was so hot that we stripped down to our underwear. Outside, it was so cold we wore down jackets."

Norbu adds, "Finally, everything was burning, so we had to get out. By then, more people arrived, having run from Pangboche and Khumjung. We shovelled snow onto the roofs of other buildings, the museum and monks' houses so they would not catch fire."

Little was left of the gonda. One strut, carved as a snow lion, fell from the corner of the building and landed in a snow bank that protected it from the flames. Five prayer wheels in a niche along the back wall of the gonda survived because a snowdrift covered them. The only mural that survived the blaze was a painting on stone of Guru Rinpoche, the founder of Mahayana Buddhism.

The fire destroyed the school building at the back of the gonda. The museum survived the blaze and became the temporary home for statues rescued from the burning gonda.

Once again the Khumbu Sherpas are reconstructing the gonda at Tengboche. This time the interest in the reconstruction is international, as individuals and organizations around the world want to contribute to the project.

Rinpoche comments, "This was a powerful place for Lama Sangwa Dorje to practise meditation. Tengboche has brought the Sherpa community together three times now to build and rebuild it. It is special."

A Sherpa living in Kathmandu describes his involvement in the reconstruction activities: "Tengboche is a very special place for the Sherpas. We love that place even if we have never been monks. Perhaps it is because the place is so beautiful, perhaps because we can see it from so many places in the Khumbu valley. It is because of these special feelings that we are all helping to reconstruct the gonda."

It was miraculous that the museum survived the fire. The top floor is the only space at Tengboche large enough for the monks to gather for prayers and ceremonies.

Ruins of gonda at Tengboche Monastery, 1989

Entering the museum's ground floor, I struggle with mixed feelings. This museum of Sherpa culture was my life and work in Nepal from 1983-88. The completed museum lasted only nine months. The fire made it necessary to dismantle the original layout to make room for the monks' religious activities on the top floor. Now, display panels from upstairs about Sherpa religion surround the exhibits about secular life downstairs. Though less organized, the arrangement is more fitting — the everyday life of the Sherpas is inseparable from religion.

A colourful Mahayana Buddhist altar still fills the end wall of the large, bright room upstairs. The monks have placed statues rescued from the burning temple on the altar and hung thankas from the gonda on the walls. Twenty monks sit on wide benches facing the centre aisle. As they chant prayers, their voices range from boyish tenor to deep bass. Two senior monks delicately clatter cymbals, while another two play a shrill melody on flutes. On cue, two young monks lift the ends of ten-foot copper horns, *sang-dung,* to their lips. A deep moan fills the room.

Rinpoche's assistant comes to take him to his house. Five foreign climbers wait on the small verandah for the ritual of securing his blessing before venturing up a mountain. The climbers and I follow Rinpoche inside. He slips off his shoes and steps up onto the carpet-covered bench stretching across the front of the room. Folding gracefully down, he sits cross-legged on the wide bench. The climbers each hand him a white ceremonial scarf, a *khata,* which he takes from their hands and places around their necks as the blessing. The climbers and I sit on benches around the room and, for an awkward moment, all look at each other.

"Do you have any questions for Rinpoche?" The climbers look surprised. The leader asks, "Have we foreigners destroyed the local peoples' culture by coming here?"

"No, not really," Rinpoche laughs. "There are outward changes in appearances: some of our dress, houses, occupations and opportunities. However, our Sherpa ceremonies and traditions — how we name children, assist the dead, get married and celebrate a year's passage — all this remains intact. What is most important to us remains. The coming of foreign visitors to Khumbu has not changed our inner culture."

After the climbers depart, I return to the gonda's ruined shell. The sounds of the prayers fade and eventually the monks emerge from the museum.

Tengboche monk reading Buddhist texts

"Namaste, when did you arrive?" Some young monks and I exchange banter, ignoring the ruins. Finally, one who worked with me on the museum, Kusang, asks, "Are you angry?"

"Well," I pause. "I have mixed feelings. The fire destroyed so much, but it impresses me how the Sherpa community has come together for the gonda's reconstruction."

"I was angry when I saw what happened," says Kusang. "Now, we will have a new gonda." We laugh despite the ruins around us. Kusang points over our heads. Late-afternoon clouds split, revealing a mountain peak 3000 metres (10,000 feet) above us. We stare as though we have never seen

Reconstructed Tengboche temple, 1993

it before. Clouds hide the mountain again and we disperse. I start back to my quarters, then quickly detour. In the heart of the ruins, the little Buddha statue provides another moment's inspiration.

Kusang was right. A year later, in April 1990, stones are broken, timbers are cut and the site is cleared and sanctified to begin construction of the new gonda. In a ceremony, the first stone for the foundation is placed in a trench. Prayers are said and speeches are made.

The feast and Sherpa line dancing continue long into the night. Wondering about the mix of religion and celebration, I remember Rinpoche's words: "Bringing people together is important because happiness is the first step on the path to enlightenment. What happens now in our hearts and minds is what is most important."

Statue of historical Buddha

Part Two

The Metaphysical and the Everyday

To Perfect Our Minds

"The purpose of our religion is to perfect our minds," says Tengboche Rinpoche. His point of view is the Buddhism of Tibet and the Himalaya, the heart and soul of the Sherpa culture.

"I was born in Nauche and as a small child talked about wanting to go home to Tengboche," says Rinpoche. He sits cross-legged on a wide bench in his dark kitchen lined with shelves of copper pots. In his lap he holds the small text from which he reads prayers every day.

"My mother carried me to Rongbuk monastery in Tibet. Upon seeing a monk, I ran to hug him as if I had known him before. He was the nephew of the founder of Tengboche. The Abbot of Rongbuk recognized me as a *tulku* [reincarnate of a spiritually advanced person], the reincarnate of Tengboche's founder, Lama Gulu.

"Back in Nauche, I identified Lama Gulu's belongings. Everyone was satisfied after this proof, so I was brought to Tengboche at the age of five to be raised as the reincarnate lama and eventually become the Abbot of the monastery."

Rinpoche spent decades studying at Tengboche and at Buddhist universities in Tibet and Darjeeling until he was ready to assume the leadership of the monastery. As a spiritual leader

Tengboche Rinpoche

of the Sherpa people, he is equally adept on matters as varied as health, education, politics, the building of bridges and the naming of children.

Rinpoche's life has been devoted to study of the Buddhist faith, which he describes by saying, "Our religion protects our character, which is why religion is so important in our culture. Happiness and unhappiness are caused by one's state of mind."

Merging the metaphysical with everyday life, the Sherpas' prayers and rituals aim to generate positive spiritual energy for the benefit of all beings. Whether layman or cleric, religion is the way of life, unifying all aspects of existence. The practice of religion is not confined to a day of the week; it is an everyday affair.

The Sherpas' religion is the oldest sect of Mahayana Buddhism, the *Nyingma,* which was established by Guru Rinpoche, an Indian mystic who was invited to establish Buddhism in Tibet about 730 CE.

Sherpa history and teachings are recorded in Tibetan script in religious books. Traditionally, these books were kept in each village temple, or gonda, where lay ministers would conduct ceremonies and teach religion.

In a typical Sherpa gonda, the main wall has shelves of religious books and statues representing the foundation of their faith. The central figure is usually the historical Buddha, who lived 2,500 years ago. He pondered the causes of suffering for many years and eventually offered teachings for spiritual development and fulfilling the potential for Buddhahood, or enlightenment, that exists within each of us.

New statue in reconstructed gonda

Another statue is *Guru Rinpoche*, who 1,200 years later developed a version of Buddhism employing mystical techniques to more quickly attain enlightenment. The third statue is usually the god of compassion, one of many deities described as a way to help enhance certain aspects of our character.

Tengboche Rinpoche introduces me to the principles and practices of Buddhism through my work to complete the Sherpa museum. He often uses examples from daily life to illustrate the complexity of Buddhism. One day, for example, talking about the Buddhist concept of emptiness:

Tengboche's monks read the scriptures of the old sect of Tibetan Buddhism, the Nyingmapa.

"Think about this knife on the table," says Rinpoche. "It's real when you are sitting here in Tengboche. Will this knife on my table be real to you in Canada? If you think about Canada right now, which is real — Canada? Or Tengboche, where your body happens to be?

"This is illusion, the unreal objects. The real objects and events happen in your mind. There are two 'rivers' to follow in our minds. The first, *Sunya*, emptiness, is about the knife. It deals with the perception or non-reality of all things. The second, *Karuna*, is compassion. After one attains perfect understanding of emptiness and compassion, one attains Buddhahood.

"This is why it is important to remember that the purpose of our religion is to improve our minds. This is why it is important to study the Buddhist teachings, think about them, meditate — and then think some more."

Meditation, the main practice of Buddhism

Two young monks in maroon robes dash into the courtyard. They each offer Rinpoche a *khata*, which he places around their necks. Rinpoche lightly blesses the tops of their heads. A khata is one of the offerings in the daily lives of the Sherpas.

I wonder how to reconcile the purpose of "perfecting our minds" with the many rituals, offerings, deities and religious objects of everyday life.

"There are many kinds of offerings," says Rinpoche. Pointing at the urn of smouldering incense hanging outside his window, he continues: "This is an offering through the sense of smell. There

Bells (tilbu) create sound offerings.

are physical offerings such as *torma* [dough figurines], visual offerings like pictures and sand mandalas, sound offerings like the ritual instruments and chants or prayers. Our good intentions are the most important offering."

Sherpa life is also full of ritual objects. Everywhere in Sherpa country are stones carved with prayers, water-driven prayer wheels, and prayer flags. The carved prayer stones usually contain a single chant, a complete prayer or a Buddhist image, while prayer wheels contain scrolls of printed prayers, often thousands of them.

Prayer flags, attached to tall poles or on strings, flutter on rooftops and mountain passes or are strung across rivers and paths. They carry printed prayers and often show the wind horse, the swift bearer of prayers. Their five colours signify the elements: earth, wood, water, fire and metal.

Turning prayer wheels is an offering that gains merit.

Stupas, called *chorten* in Sherpa and Tibetan, are the numerous monuments found across the Buddhist countryside by paths, streams, homes and gondas. Chorten represent the body, mind and spiritual development of the Buddha.

During the historical Buddha's lifetime, stupas were memorials for the deceased. As the Buddha lay dying, his followers asked what should be done with his remains. He requested that his body be placed in a simple stupa. Since then, the stupa has symbolized the Buddha, and often offerings or the relics of the deceased, especially of lamas, are sealed inside various sizes and shapes of stupas.

While discussing displays for the museum, Rinpoche explains the importance of Buddhist prayers on rocks, flags and other objects: "We see them everywhere in the land of Buddhist

Lhachetup, the ritual to protect the home with prayer flags on the roof

people. These religious objects are part of our daily lives. They help focus people's thoughts on the Buddhist teachings and bring about a positive state of mind in people, to the benefit of all.

"The religious objects help create harmony between our actions, body and mind. The Buddhist teachings will come easily to us when we gain merit first with our actions and body and then through our minds. So that everyone may understand them, religious objects have many explanations at these different levels."

These objects allow anyone to gain spiritual merit through good intentions and each flutter of the prayer flag or turn of the prayer wheel.

PLACES OF POWER

Prayer flags flutter at a notch in a jagged, rocky ridge. Our group of Sherpas and foreign trekkers has made its way carefully down the narrow track made slippery by snow, ice and mud.

At the pass is a cairn with prayer flags, a *labtsa*. Each Sherpa companion places a small stone from the path onto the cairn, giving thanks that our trekking group has safely finished this part of our journey. I follow suit.

Farther down the trail we turn our backs to gusts of wind. In the fury of blowing dust, we hide our faces inside our jackets. Though I see only the ground before me, a vision fills my mind — a hard impact on the back of my head and then a sudden void.

I react by taking two steps forward…

In that instant, a thick board blown off a nearby hut hits the back of my ankle. Shocked, I feel the pain in my ankle ebbing with the realization that the board would have struck my head if I had not stepped forward.

After the incident, Sherpa friends explain my premonition. "*Khumbila*, our local mountain god, protects all of us in this Khumbu valley. He may have sent the vision to help you move from harm's way."

Two weeks later, I ask Tengboche Rinpoche about the suggestion that the incident was protection from Khumbila. He is quiet for several minutes and then says, "Yes, Khumbila helped you by bringing that insight. This means of protection works for the Sherpas because we understand the power of this place. Although you are not Sherpa, you have lived here long enough."

For years, I have heard of Khumbila, the spiritual guardian of Khumbu, but I have never really understood how he protected the valley's inhabitants. Wondering about recent disasters, I ask, "How about the giant flood last year? Where was Khumbila then?"

"The flood reminded us to cherish our land. It was going to happen, but very few people were killed. Perhaps Khumbila's influence held the flood until a day when many people were at

Khumbila, the protector of the Khumbu valley

a festival high in the yak pastures. Imagine if the flood had happened in October when the trails by the river would have been crowded with Sherpas, porters and trekkers. Khumbila protected us from that disaster.

"Khumbila cannot protect everyone from everything. His protection depends on karma, the impending consequences of our behaviour. If your work here was without merit, if you had not been open to our Sherpa way of seeing the world, you may not have been able to see the vision Khumbila offered."

As a Westerner, I had tried at first to intellectually understand this other way of seeing the world. Being with people with different perceptions and assumptions, I gradually learned to perceive and accept other cultures and ways of life. The total immersion in Sherpa culture led not to a rejection of my culture, but to a realization that other ways of being work for people in different geographic situations.

The people of the Himalaya believe the mountain peaks, ridges, passes, fields and homes are the abodes of deities representing the power of the place. The prayer flags, ceremonies and little rituals of everyday life in these places acknowledge some greater power.

The Sherpas' lives embrace extremes: folk belief and a profound spirituality, loneliness and social obligation, deprivation and abundance. The existence of one extreme doesn't rule out the possibility of its opposite.

For the Sherpas, Khumbila is the short name of the *Khumbu-yul-lha*, "Khumbu country-god." He is the protector of the land, people and religion of the Khumbu. He is shown riding a great white horse and carrying a tall banner. Rinpoche says, "Khumbila wears the traditional turban-like headgear that men wore in the old days. When I was a boy, the mountain had a ring of snow, like the headdress, at its summit."

Rinpoche tells how the Sherpas' ancestors brought books from Tibet describing the mountain and a valley that would be a refuge for people fleeing trouble in Tibet. At the centre of this valley is the mountain Khumbila, the abode of the protector deity.

Sherpas and Tibetans also believe that Everest is the abode of the goddess *Jomo Miyo*

Jomo Miyo Langsangma resides on Everest.

Langsangma. This lovely resident of the earth's highest place is one of the five Long-life Sisters inhabiting peaks of the Himalaya. Tengboche Rinpoche describes her: "She is the goddess of humans and rides a red tiger. Miyo Langsangma is very pretty. Her skin is orange and bright, flowers wreathe her head, and she wears many colours of silk cloth. She holds a long bowl of food in her right hand and a mongoose that spits out wealth in her left."

Legends say this goddess distributes wealth and good fortune. In modern times, expeditions and treks to Everest have brought affluence to many Sherpas. At the start of each expedition, Sherpa crews perform rituals to appease the goddess before entering her abode.

The Khumbu Icefall above Everest Base Camp

The Tengboche monks are conscious that the ridge where the monastery sits is the abode of a minor female deity, a *lhamo*. This day is the annual ritual at the cairn on the ridge to honour the goddess of this place.

The ridge above Tengboche is 900 metres (3,000 feet) higher than the main Khumbu villages and surrounded by mountains. It rises from forested slopes to a jagged summit plastered with finely fluted snow. At a low crest of the ridge is a large cairn with prayer flags. This *lhapso* is a monument acknowledging the power there.

Today, the monks are preparing new flags to place on the lhapso. In the gonda courtyard, two monks are printing flags. The first monk brushes ink onto a wooden block etched with the reverse imprint of a religious image. He positions a piece of cotton on the block and holds it in place while the other monk runs a roller over the cloth. The image prints onto the fabric. Two older monks stitch the flags onto long bamboo sticks.

Two young monks bound back into the courtyard after the twenty-minute trip up and down the mountainside to deliver flags to the lhapso site.

Each boy grips another armload of bamboo poles against his chest, gingerly balancing the sticks twice as tall as himself. As the boys

Stitching flags onto long bamboo sticks

scuffle up the hill, they are careful not to desecrate the flags by letting them touch the ground.

Monks carry low tables, cushions, ritual instruments and Thermoses of tea up the ridge. They arrange the cushions and tables along the edge of the forest. A middle-aged monk places sculptures of *tsampa* (barley flour) and butter, called *torma*, on a ledge on the cairn. The flat ground by the lhapso becomes an outdoor temple.

This lhapso is a stone and plaster cairn six feet high. Standing on top, the prayer leader removes old flags and carefully pushes the new flags' bamboo poles into its earthen top. Other monks pile the old flags and green juniper boughs onto a smouldering fire. Fragrant smoke billows from the

Placing new prayer flags on the power place above Tengboche

A sacred site near Pangboche, with Everest and Lhotse behind

juniper. It signals that the ceremony is ready to start. Half an hour later all the monks finally arrive at the site.

The monks sit facing Khumbila to the west, across the gorge from Tengboche. Behind them, large yellow rhododendron blooms cover the trees. The monks blow horns, clatter cymbals and chant prayers to the deity of the ridge, who personifies the power of this place.

In the ceremony, Rinpoche recites the prayers with intense concentration. Afterward, he describes the prayers: "The prayers connect the spiritual with the physical. Our thoughts connect with the power of nature. We restore the harmony between us, nature and spiritual beings."

Creating harmony with the environment through prayers at Tengboche

It is not easy living in these mountains. On the narrow trails or in the fields, the immense power of the land can harm or kill. Sherpas do not tame nature; they accommodate this power that is beyond their control. Ceremonies to harmonize humans and nature give people a way to understand their environment.

Sherpas explain the power of their environment through a view that everything exists in two forms: the physical and the spiritual. They may see a god either as a real personality living on a mountaintop or as a symbol of nature's power.

Their beliefs embrace tiers of explanations with deeper and deeper meanings, but all these rituals and objects of everyday life — the ceremonies, prayer flags and mani stones — acknowledge some greater power.

Kantega with mani stones, near Pangboche

To quote Tibetan writer Thubten Jigme Norbu:[1]

"You find prayer flags on hills, mountains, by lakes and always on the crest of passes. It does not really matter whether these spirits exist. What matters is that through these stories we have come to believe that everywhere, all around us, at all times, there is some power that is greater than ourselves."

The ritual on the mountainside draws to a close, as the monks' prayers and horns merge with the whistle of the wind. Smouldering juniper incense mingles with wispy clouds condensing around the mountainside.

As chants and wind seem to merge the metaphysical and the everyday, I appreciate that moment when a metaphysical being might have intervened in my everyday life.

1 Norbu and Turnbull, p. 32.

Some power greater than ourselves: glaciers on Nuptse

Rinpoche describes the rituals: "The prayers connect our thoughts with the power of nature."

BEYUL:
THE SACRED VALLEY

"This valley is sacred to us Sherpa," says Rinpoche. "The only way to come or leave here is to climb over a very high pass or to trudge up the steep gorge of the Dudh Kosi river. We live in a protected place."

Rinpoche then recites Sherpa narratives describing how special spiritual powers have been used twice to create a *beyul*, a sacred sanctuary, in the Khumbu valley — first to sanctify it and then to open it as a sanctuary.

"One of our religious texts foretold that in the future … the religious people would have to run away to secluded mountain valleys described in religious texts."

When helping to establish Buddhism in Tibet, Guru Rinpoche predicted there would be times of trouble when some people in the Tibetan region would have to flee their homes. He also sanctified and hid many valleys in the Himalaya to serve as sanctuaries.

Guru Rinpoche instructed some of his pupils to write guidebooks which were later hidden in the rocks and earth. These hidden teachings would offer directions on how to get to the sanctuaries. In times of trouble, various inspired lamas and their devout followers would be able to find these places by following the directions in the books.

The Khumbu valley is one of these hidden sacred sanctuaries, these beyuls.

"When there were troubles hundreds of years ago, we know that the ancestors of the present-day Sherpas left Kham in far-eastern Tibet because it was against their religious belief to fight. They moved westward along the north side of the Himalaya.

"They were looking for a beyul, a sanctuary, because the lamas leading them were following the directions recorded in a religious text. The lamas needed not only the skills to read and understand the book, but also the spiritual power to recognize clues in the landscape, in order to discover the beyul."

Guru Rinpoche painting on a cliff face

The Khumbu valley, with Jomolungma (Everest), Khunde and Khumjung villages and Ama Dablam

The Sherpa ancestors crossed the Himalaya through a pass to the west of Khumbu. They started small homesteads lower down near present-day Lukla. The first Sherpa to enter the beyul, Phachhen, struggled to walk up the wild canyon, clambering up and down around cliffs, boulders and trees. Eventually, several families settled on the warm slopes below the present villages in the upper valley, the Khumbu beyul.

"When Phachhen, the first Sherpa, arrived in Khumbu around five or six hundred years ago, the valley was covered by snow and the glaciers were much bigger than they are now. Gradually the snow and ice melted."

Sherpas use the high mountainsides of the beyul as pastures.

Khumbu is not the first or the last beyul to serve as a sanctuary in the Himalaya. Others have been located across the high Himalaya of Nepal, Tibet, China, India, Bhutan and Pakistan. To the southeast of Khumbu, the beyul of Khenpalung has yet to be opened for the devout.

I ask Rinpoche about an American scholar who organized an expedition that succeeded in crossing several high passes to enter Khenpalung. Rinpoche responds:

"He found the way into Khenpalung, the physical place, but did not see the real inside place. Our friend was not the right person, it was not the right time, and the team did not have the spiritual preparation to see all that was there. For a beyul to be revealed, the directions to find it must be followed by the right group of people with strong faith and pure motives.

The first Sherpa to enter Khumbu walked up the rugged canyon.

"So it is with the beyul: we see and hear part of what is there, but we miss certain things because we aren't ready or able to perceive them. The inside of the mandala was invisible to them."

I wonder how to interpret Rinpoche's remarks. Perhaps being spiritually unprepared is like being tone-deaf: certain notes just do not register. The fact that the Khenpalung beyul has been physically entered but not spiritually found suggests that it is not a place where we must go on foot.

Is a true beyul a place that we find in our minds? We need spiritual power, like Phachhen's, to thwart the demons of greed, ignorance and desire that will obstruct our path. But the path is there. It takes only determination and courage to follow it. The beyul is an inside place, a spiritual sanctuary. "The most important beyul is in our minds," says Rinpoche.

When the Sherpas first came, ice and snow covered much of Khumbu.

Religious objects, such as prayer flags and khatas, have tiers of meanings.

THE GODS WITHIN YOU

A letter arrives saying that a friend in Canada has been killed in an accident. It asks me to arrange to have some prayers done for Nina.

The monks at Tengboche are busy, but someone suggests the *anis* (nuns) at Devuche, the little nunnery twenty minutes' walk away. Devuche sits in a meadow at the edge of the rhododendron forest in a quiet, peaceful place.

At Devuche, I arrange for the anis to say some prayers the next day. However, in the morning, only the abbess and one elderly nun are present in the kitchen.

The abbess hands me some of the 50-rupee notes I had given her the day before. "Take this to the blind ani, who can't come do the puja (prayers) in the gonda but can say prayers. Take this to the ani in this house right here, who is in retreat."

I knock on the door of the ani in retreat. An elderly person wearing robes and a traditional winged yellow hat opens the door. I ask, "Would you please say some prayers for a friend of mine who died 49 days ago?" She gestures for me to enter. Her small home is clean and tidy. I sit on a wide bench stretching across the end of the room while she prepares tea on the little clay-lined, one-pot burner. She asks the name of my friend who has died. "Ni-na," she repeats as she notes it down in Tibetan script on an envelope.

"How long have you been in retreat?" I ask.

"Twenty years," she pauses, "and thirteen years. For this time, I have not left this little compound.

"I am from Nauche. My family did business in Tibet. When I was eight years old, I first went to Rongbuk. There I received a blessing from Zatul Rinpoche and took my first vows to become an ani with Tulshi Rinpoche.

"When I was twenty, I was here in Devuche and had been an ani for several years. A rich man from Solu wanted another wife after his first passed away. He first sent one and then two men from Solu to Nauche to ask my mother in Nauche while my father was in Tibet trading. She sent them away.

"Then, he got several men together — about eleven of them just to come get one woman. They surrounded my house here in Devuche. I went to bed but could not sleep. Finally, I escaped out a window late at night and hid in the river gorge.

"They looked in the woods and all the houses. I hid by the river for two days and on the second night wondered what to do. I had no food, no shoes, just the robe I grabbed as I crawled out of bed.

"Finally, I worked my way along the river and up through the forest to Tengboche. Rinpoche could not hide me there, because monastery rules do not allow women to stay.

"A man who had just come from Tibet a year before agreed to help me. We hid in the day and travelled at night through Thame and over the pass to Tibet. In those days it took four days to walk across the Nangpa *La* (pass) to the first village in Tibet, then ten days to Shigatse and ten more to Lhasa. I stayed there for ten years until I was thirty.

"When the Chinese became really strong in Tibet, I was studying at a nunnery higher in a valley. Rinpoche and his half-brothers were at a monastery nearby. They came to see me. We decided it was time to return to Nepal. I came to Devuche and started my retreat.

"For six weeks after I arrived here in Devuche, we did not know if the Dalai Lama was alive or dead. Then finally one day I heard that he was in Kalimpong. What a relief." As I stand up to leave, I pull another 50-rupee note from my wallet.

"Would you also please do some prayers for the book I'm working on?"

Ani-la holds the bill thoughtfully for a moment before setting it on the windowsill among her papers.

"People always come and ask me to say prayers for this and for that. So their son will get into this school or that this business venture will be successful. They do not understand that when these prayers bring about general good fortune or merit, it comes from within, from within themselves."

A memorial and mani stones in the quiet forest near Devuche

She hands me a paper and a pen.

"I want you to write down these prayers so you can say them yourself for good things to happen. *Om Ah Hung Betza Guru Padme Siti Hung* is to Guru Rinpoche. The next is *Om Mani Padme Hung* to Chyenrezig. *Om Ah Mi De Wa Hri* to Opagme."

I obediently write down the mantras as she hovers above me in her winged cap.

"Say 108 of each mantra. Say them every day if you can. As you say them, always think of going to the place of the gods, but always remember…"

She reaches out and touches my chest. "Always remember that the gods are right here within you."

Winnowing grain is a time-consuming activity.

Part Three

Rhythms of the Year

❧

Everyday Life

Daylight breaks with the sloshing sounds of tea being churned. Within minutes, seven-year-old Yangjin arrives with a heavy Thermos, which she sets in the middle of the floor to pour a cup of tea.

In all Sherpa households, tea is always available and consumed constantly throughout each day. The tea is prepared early every morning and stored in a Thermos.

Tea served by a smiling seven-year-old compensates for the many inconveniences of living at Tengboche in the mid-1980s — the lack of indoor toilets, running water, phones and electricity. The monastery laws prohibit women from living within the monastic complex, so I stay at the lodge of Yangjin's parents, Pasang and Nyisha.

Yangjin practises the alphabet she learned at school on a blank piece of paper on my desk. Tengboche has a monastic school for boys, but nothing for girls. Her parents enrolled her at the school in Khumjung, where she stays with an aunt during school sessions. She is learning Nepali, arithmetic, health, social studies and rudimentary English, although her "trekking" English is already polished.

Operated by the government, this school does not teach these children their Sherpa language, culture or history. It must close for Hindu holidays, but not Sherpa ones, when many children have to miss classes.

The morning tea comes with milk and sugar already added as an adaptation of the British tea served in India. The traditional-style tea preferred by the Sherpas consists of a brew from dark tea leaves mixed in a churn with butter and rock salt.

Nyisha brings a small bowl of tsampa, the roasted-barley-flour staple of Himalayan people. It keeps for months dry and is usually mixed with tea or butter to make porridge or little blocks that are easily carried and eaten on the trail.

Later, Yangjin decides to come along as I prepare to walk to Pangboche to interview and photograph an old man who still carves prayer stones.

On the trail, we follow tracks to the left of the many mani stones along the trail. An older Sherpa woman catches up with us. "Let's walk together," she says. On the trails, people like to walk together. Having deliberately caught up to us for company, she is disappointed that we are not going far. While walking, she spins the fleece wrapped around her wrist by rolling a spindle down her thigh and letting the weight of the spinning spindle twist the fleece into yarn.

Farther on, clattering bells warn us to move to the side of the narrow track as a train of yaks and *zopkyoks* (a crossbreed of yak and cow) passes, loaded with the brightly coloured duffel bags of a trekking group. Their driver whistles and shrieks to urge the animals forward.

In Pangboche, the stone carver describes how fine-grained stones are easier to carve than coarse-grained ones. In the midst of his description, he interjects bits of local gossip, calls over the fence to a neighbour and argues with his wife.

When we arrive back at Tengboche, Nyisha hands me a box. "Can you sort through this? Most is in English, so I don't know what might be useful for the museum."

Dawa Tenzing's invitation to the coronation of Queen Elizabeth II and portrait

I peek into the dusty box. On top is a book on the 1953 Everest expedition, when Edmund Hillary and Sherpa Tenzing Norgay made the first successful ascent of Everest. Inside the cover are the autographs of all the expedition members. Nyisha's father, Dawa Tenzing, was the sardar on the historic 1953 expedition.

Deep in the box are photographs of Dawa and various Westerners. In gratitude for his services, the expedition members took him to England. Dawa wore Western dress in some photographs and traditional Sherpa garb in others, including one of him meeting a young Queen Elizabeth. Regardless of his dress, he wore his long hair in braids wrapped around his head.

The Alpine Club had awarded Dawa a lifetime membership, so he had received all the mail, from annual reports to advertisements for electric kettles and cars.

Dawa was particularly fond of Tengboche and spent his days circling the monastery. It was fortunate that his daughter had a hotel here.

Late that night in the kitchen, Pasang is talking with a Nepali hill man with grey hair and rough, worn hands. Pasang says, "This is the *kami* [metalworker] from Nauche. He has brought some new instruments for the monastery."

The kamis are one of the many occupational castes in the Hindu hierarchy, in which they are regarded as "untouchable." Some Sherpa households will follow the Hindu tradition of not letting people from these castes into their homes. Others, like Pasang, rightly refused to follow these traditions of the "down valley" people.

In the dim light of a wick lamp, the man tells his story. "My grandfather came to work in Nauche long ago. He came from the hills south of here when some of the people who had lots of money from trading in Tibet were building new houses, gondas and stupas.

"My grandfather came here to make metal horns, instruments and *sentoks*, the golden spires on top of gondas and stupas. He made the one on the first gonda here at Tengboche. His work was so good that he became famous and was invited to work in Tibet. One night, while working on the sentok at Rongbuk monastery on the north side of Everest, he suddenly died. No one knows why. He just died.

"But our family has stayed in Nauche ever since. There are four kami families now because we have so much work." He pulls a bundle from his bag and unwraps an exquisite *sangshu*, a kettle for water offerings. The joins in the copper bowl are almost invisible and the filigree work is fine and finished.

"It took about a month to make this," he says. "I like making these instruments for religious rituals. I like their purpose."

"Eat Potatoes, Dig Potatoes"

Puffs of dust follow each blow of the hoe. Lhamu swings the hoe high above her shoulders and lets it arc downward, breaking the black earth of the stone-walled field. Her sister, Pema, holds a small basket from which she tosses a piece of old potato into each fresh cleft.

Across the field, their six-year-old niece sings a high-pitched Sherpa folk song to Lhamu's infant daughter, who lies bundled in a rectangular basket.

Lhamu wears her oldest ankle-length *ungi*, a Sherpa dress, over a thinning American Everest expedition T-shirt. Around her head she has wrapped a faded pink towel, tied at the back over her long, thick black braid. As I approach with my camera, Lhamu and Pema stop their work. Understandably, Sherpas do not like having their photographs taken while working in the fields. This is dirty work and they are dressed accordingly.

Lhamu's hands show signs of toil: black soil covering cracked, rough skin.

Here at the edge of the inhabitable, the work for food is arduous. Fields that yield only a single harvest of potatoes or buckwheat each year seem to produce perpetual crops of pebbles and stones. Sherpas carved these flat terraces out of the thin, dry soil on the mountainsides. At this high altitude, the climate leaves little frost-free time in which to grow crops of potatoes, buckwheat or barley.

"When did the frozen waterfall fall this spring?" I ask as we walk lightly over the loose soil to where Lhamu's baby howls with hunger.

"Last week," she responds while excavating the baby from within layers of blankets. We sit cross-legged on the ground while she breastfeeds her child. Sherpas know the soil is warm enough to start planting potatoes from many natural signs, such as when irises bloom, when the sun rises through a certain notch in the mountains, or when a massive frozen waterfall melts and cascades down to the canyon below.

Sherpas spend days weeding potato fields during the monsoon.

"We broke and turned the soil in our fields earlier this week and have to plant the potatoes before it dries out," explains Lhamu. "Last week we hired a couple of boys from way down-valley to carry the compost to the fields."

This task is unpleasant but necessary. Sherpas fertilize their fields with animal waste from their barns or toilet waste from the traditional latrines situated next to many homes. Each latrine has a large supply of leaves, collected from the forest in the fall. At the conclusion of a visit, one kicks a few leaves down the hole. The mixture below is half leaf litter. Mixed into the fields, it adds greatly to the fertility of the mediocre soil.

A ritual called *Orsho* marks the beginning of the agricultural season. A procession of villagers and lay lamas circles the village fields. Two men blow conch shells while a third beats a large round drum held vertically by a wooden handle.

At cairns on the fields, the group makes offerings, erects prayer flags and recites prayers. To Sherpas, the power of the land is focused and accessible at these cairns.

The villagers build a spiritual boundary reinforcing the stonewalls protecting the fields. This boundary is to keep out bad spirits or negative energy that could bring disaster to the crops. The ritual protects the fields in another way, too, for it asserts the community's right to prevent livestock from grazing in the village and thus protects the crops from being devoured by the wandering animals.

Lhamu describes her family's division of labour. Her eldest brother has taken their small herd to a pasture a day's walk away. Another brother is away working on a climbing expedition. She, her mother and her sister are planting potatoes in April to be harvested in September.

A group of women passes by, taking a break from their work in a nearby field.

"Hey, Lhamu, do you have a *meek-karu* [literally "white-eyes," slang for white person] helper today?" shouts one of them. We laugh.

The sound of the other women's giggling follows them down the trail. Pema brings another basket of seed potatoes stored from the previous harvest.

Seed potatoes are stored in pits in the ground.

"We spent all day yesterday sorting and cutting seed potatoes. Our mother is still doing it today. We don't take too many potatoes out of the hole at once."

Lhamu refers to the four-foot-deep holes dug in the fields in front of houses to store potatoes over the winter. Sherpas line the holes with branches of juniper and pile soil on top of the potatoes to keep them fresh through the winter.

Her mother soon joins us, carrying a large handle-less pot. She lifts a lid, releasing a cloud of steam. The boiled potatoes in the pot have smooth, wet, dark-brown skins. Pema places a bowl

Potatoes are planted and harvested by hand.

of mashed chilies, chives, garlic and yogourt next to the pot. She grabs a potato, squeezes it out of its skin, breaks it into bite-sized pieces and dips the first piece into the bowl's spicy mixture.

Between mouthfuls, she says, "Of all the ways that we Sherpas prepare potatoes, this simple way is how I like them best. Please have some."

The mother notices me examining the different kinds of seed potatoes in the basket. "We grow three kinds of *rigis* [potatoes] in Khumbu now. Most people like the little red ones, called *rigi moru*, the best. The other, long yellow potatoes, *rigi seru*, don't taste as good but produce a much greater harvest. Another kind of potato, brought here by the government a few years ago, won't grow in Khumbu."

When everyone has had their fill, we pack up the half-empty pot and bowl.

"Tonight we will use these leftover potatoes to make *rildok sen* [a thick potato mash eaten with cheese soup]."

Lhamu uses a long, narrow basket as a crib on the ground or as a baby carrier when suspended on her back by a tumpline around the corners of the basket. She puts her back up to the basket and places the line over her head. As she stands up, the basket hangs by the line over her head and rests against her back. Shuffling and rocking the baby to sleep, Lhamu picks up the basket of cut potatoes and trades jobs with her sister.

She rocks the baby and tosses potatoes, doing two jobs at once. I pick and toss the newest crop of rocks from the field. Her sister swings the hoe fast and hard. Each strike of the hoe in the earth produces a fine cloud of black dust that gradually coats us from head to toe.

"In a few weeks, this dirty field will be green with little potato plants," says Lhamu, "Then we'll sit in the fields to pull the weeds."

"When the potato plants are this high, we cut and dry them." Lhamu gestures to the middle of her thigh. "The dried plants are fed to the yaks in winter. We use everything." She pauses as she and her sister swing around in unison to start another row. "Then we dig in the dirt again to find the new potatoes. Eat potatoes, dig potatoes," she laughs. "Dig potatoes, eat potatoes."

TRADE AND MARKETS

Wangmu left without me. To shop for her family's hotel, she leaves early each Saturday to walk three hours and arrive at the weekly market in Nauche in time for the best deals.

People from some villages must walk four or five hours each way to the market. Some do the return trip in a single day.

Trails leading into the bazaar are steady streams of people. By the south entry to the village, hundreds of people are crowded onto the three terraces where the market is held. Sherpas and other residents of Khumbu, such as Nepali officials, police and schoolteachers, or foreign researchers, squeeze between rows of vendors squatting by their baskets of wares.

A Sherpa woman carefully examines rice grains and says, "Two paathis." A *paathi* equals about four litres. "*Ek, ek, ek, dui, dui, dui, dui, tin, tin, tin...*" the vendor counts out measures of wheat into a brass vessel and dumps the grain into the woman's open bag. Everyone brings containers and bags for their purchases.

An elderly Sherpa man wears a *chuba* (robe) and the traditional headdress of a wide sash wrapped around his head. He tests the next vendor's rice by popping a few grains in his mouth.

A butcher weighs out portions of water-buffalo meat. He walked the animal up the trail and slaughtered it yesterday in the forest below Nauche. Sherpas sell water buffalo as "yak" steak in the tourist hotels and joke about calling it "lowland" yak.

They rarely slaughter yaks for meat, unless the animal is injured. The male yaks are too valuable as pack animals, and the female *naks* give milk. An irony is that while Sherpas, as Buddhists, will not themselves slaughter an animal for meat, they will purchase and eat meat if someone else has killed the animal.

Finally, I find fresh peas and carrots. Fresh vegetables are just now available after a long winter. Next to the girls, a young Nauche woman sells powdered milk.

The market in Nauche is held throughout the year.

Merchants selling soap, kerosene, mustard oil, tea, plasticware, beer and soft drinks occupy the entire lower terrace. Vendors and porters carry loads of these goods through the heat of the lower elevations. Some carry loads well over 80 kilograms (175 pounds), moving in 20-metre (65-foot) spurts on the uphill.

Many vendors and porters are Rai people from southeast of Khumbu. They live in rugged, steep terrain rarely visited by outsiders or foreigners. Between planting and harvesting their rice and millet crops, Rai villagers may bring a load of surplus grain to sell at the bazaar or work carrying a load to Nauche for merchants.

In the cool breeze, a young porter shivers in his thin cotton clothing and bare legs and feet. Most porters camp at the bottom of the Nauche hill and scurry up in the morning. Once their goods are sold, they dash down to the relative warmth of the river gorge.

Weekly markets take place throughout Nepal, but are not a Sherpa tradition. This market was started by a government administrator in the mid-1960s to meet the needs of the growing population of civil servants stationed there. Thus, Nauche became *Namche Bazaar*.

The Sherpas were once middlemen in the trade between Tibet and northern India. Until the mid-1960s, many Nauche Sherpa traders would stockpile salt and wool from Tibet in their homes until they could exchange it for rice and grains in Nepal and India.

I recall Khonjo Chombi (the adviser for the museum) saying, "My father traded throughout eastern Nepal and to Darjeeling in India." Khonjo Chombi had a big plastic bag of folded papers, some written in Nepali script and others in Tibetan. One document was dated 1828.

"This paper from the government in Kathmandu granted us Sherpas a monopoly on the trade route between Nepal and Tibet over the Nangpa La pass. It allowed only Khumbu people to cross the glacier-covered pass."

One friend's father continued trading in Tibet until his death in 1990. He bought zopkyoks, snuff and buffalo skins in Nepal.

Rai people from lower valleys bring grain to sell at the market.

The market on Saturdays is a busy event.

In Tibet he would trade one zopkyok for three loads of sheep's wool that was worth almost four zopkyoks back in Khumbu. He would barter two or three bottles of snuff for three or four kilograms of rock salt. He also brought the cotton string and gauze required for making prayer flags to Tibet from India.

The traders took about eight days to walk to markets in Tibet, depending on the weather and the conditions on the way. It took a full day to cross the glacier, and the passage of so many heavily laden yaks had worn paths in the ice. Although Sherpas rarely trade in Tibet now, more Tibetans are crossing the pass bringing salt, meat and manufactured goods from China.

Meanwhile at the bazaar, four Tibetans sell their wares at the end of a terrace. One wears a sheepskin jacket and pants that resemble his face made leathery by a lifetime of exposure to wind and cold. The younger men wear the same jackets with corduroy or wool pants. They all wear long braids tied with long red tassels wrapped around their heads.

In brown paper wrappings are bricks of dark Chinese tea leaves used to make the traditional tea with salt and butter. Woven yak's-wool bags are rolled back to reveal the Tibetan rock salt that Sherpas still prefer in their food and tea despite its lack of iodine.

The Tibetans also sell dried legs of sheep meat, which Sherpas chop and add to stews, soups and curried potato dishes. A Sherpa woman haggles with a Tibetan as he weighs sheep lard on a balance made of a stick, a stone and leather thongs.

Finally, I take a break in a teashop. In walks Wangmu. We laugh at each other. Although we did not walk together this morning, at least we can have tea together. She orders plates of *momos* (dumplings) for two friends and us. I tell her I have already eaten, but she insists. This is her day to manage the family purse strings.

Leaving the teahouse, I look for Wangmu but she is long gone up the trail.

High Green Valleys:
Summer in Khumbu

The tiny settlement appears deserted. Except for a few shaggy yaks, everyone has retreated indoors during the afternoon rain.

Heavy mist blankets the mountainside where I follow an overgrown trail between stone walls. The mist and the thick, damp grass muffle all sound as I search for the stone hut where I am invited to spend the night.

An elderly woman appears in the fading light, wading toward me through a field of wildflowers and grass. It is a relief to see my friend's mother, Ama Yangjin. In the Sherpa language, *ama* means mother. Everyone calls her that out of respect and affection. She carefully sets down her slender wooden milking buckets and waves for me to follow her.

I bend over double to enter the tiny door of her hut and leave my damp pack in the anteroom, where supplies and the remnants of last year's hay are stored. In the main room, wide benches that double as beds line the walls around the hearth.

Ama Yangjin pours milk from the wooden buckets into a large metal pot and quickly prepares us tea. Sitting quietly by the hearth, we are warm and dry.

In the valleys of Khumbu, the summer monsoon lasts from June to September. During this quiet but productive season, people carry out their herding and farming chores with calm dignity and quiet purpose.

Farming is not easy on these mountains, but most Sherpas own plots of land at relatively low elevations below 3800 metres (12,500 feet) where they grow potatoes, buckwheat or barley to help feed their families. In summer, herders take their yaks to high valleys where the rains transform dry mountainsides into lush, green pastures.

Ama Yangjin leaving her summer hut to go milk her livestock.

Summer rains colour these valleys unimaginable hues of green. Wildflowers carpet the hillsides. Many days dawn clear. The hills vibrate with colour and the mountains sparkle with fresh snow.

Clouds form rapidly to shroud the peaks by noon. Mist becomes drizzle, which by late afternoon is rain. People time their activities to the daily weather patterns, retreating indoors as the afternoon rain begins.

Despite the weather, this is a favourite season for most Sherpas. Those who have moved to Kathmandu wistfully long for the cool, green mountain monsoon. Since most visitors avoid travelling in Nepal in the monsoon, those who work as guides and porters return to their homes in the high country.

Here in this high valley, I listen to the gentle rush of wind outside. Ama Yangjin offers a bowl of boiled potatoes.

The pace of her days in the summer pasture is steady and predictable — fetching her animals, milking the females, heating the milk and making it into yogourt and butter. Between her herding chores, she fetches water, cooks, and looks after her grandchildren.

This maze of fields, stone walls and huts is an oasis of habitation amid isolated valleys at 4300 metres (14,000 feet). Several families have summer pastures for their yak herds here. The shaggy bovines provide dairy products, wool, transportation, and a good excuse to spend three months in these mountain meadows.

From her main house in the village far below, Ama Yangjin has brought just enough for her simplest needs. Only essential kitchen utensils line the shelves.

Though she stays in the hut alone, her eldest son and his wife and children inhabit another hut nearby. They help Ama Yangjin with her heavier chores and she keeps an eye on the younger grandchildren. They visit several times a day. Conversation and sharing a few moments together seem just as important as tending the herds.

Her hands are busy even as she sits chatting. Everyone learns to spin wool and works at it continuously during the monsoon. Wool is plucked from the yaks in the spring, then beaten and rolled by hand into loops, which are coarsely spun by the men. Women usually do the final, fine spinning. Eventually the yarn is woven into long, narrow panels that are sewn together to make blankets.

As we prepare to sleep, Ama Yangjin spreads out a striped brown and grey blanket for me in case my sleeping bag is not warm enough.

In the morning, she rises before dawn to start the fire and brew the traditional butter salt tea. I listen to the rhythmic sound of the long, narrow tea churn.

After three cups of tea, we venture out to the corral, where she has tethered her female animals and their young for the night. "How much milk does a yak give each day?" I ask.

Ama Yangjin laughs. "Yaks don't give milk," she chuckles even more. "Yaks are the males. We call the females naks. That's why we always laugh when foreigners ask for yak cheese."

She deftly binds the rear legs of a slightly perturbed nak. Talking gently, she squats beside it and coaxes the milk from its udders into the wooden bucket.

She carefully describes the gender and parentage of her animals: three yaks, seven naks, ten *yakbees* (the young of the species) and several zopkyoks — male crossbreeds that are sterile and are used as pack animals, especially on trips down to the warmer elevations, which pure yaks cannot tolerate. In the trekking season, her male animals may be hired out to carry trekkers' loads. These shaggy creatures are a good investment of the family's earnings from trade or tourism. Female crosses are called zoms. They produce greater amounts of milk that is almost as rich as a nak's.

Ama Yangjin explains how she first makes the milk into yogourt so it will keep for three or four days until she has collected enough to churn it into butter.

"The butter has to be churned enough to squeeze out all the buttermilk. Then it should keep without smelling for a year. In a good summer, I might make enough butter for my family's needs and have some extra to sell to a tourist hotel in Nauche."

Fields of wildflowers are cut for hay.

The female crossbreed of a yak and a cow produces greater volumes of milk.

Naks, female yaks, provide milk for yogourt and butter.

Owning a herd necessitates having pastures away from the main villages. Some families move from their spacious homes in the main villages in late June just as the rains begin. They may have huts at three or four monsoon grazing areas. Ama Yangjin explains:

"Our traditional Sherpa rules prohibit us from keeping livestock at the main villages during the summer while the crops are growing. It's in everyone's interest not to have animals breaking into fields to devour the crops. A hungry yak can make a mess of a potato field.

"We shift our herds to a new pasture at least twice in the monsoon. It depends on the size of the valley and on when the grass is at its prime in each place."

By fall, the herds graze the mountainside pastures low. Some fields are walled to protect grass that is cut for hay to feed livestock during the winter. The field in front of Ama Yangjin's hut is knee-deep with pale blue fleabanes, golden ragwort and bright yellow cinquefoil. A tiny track leads through the wildflowers.

The morning is clear and bright — good conditions to cut and dry grass for hay. The eldest son and his wife wield a scythe in each hand, mowing the grass close to the ground. Ama Yangjin and her two older grandchildren follow with wooden rakes, gathering the cut grass and piling it into stacks. The air is full of the scent of freshly cut grass.

The grass cutting draws to a close as the afternoon drizzle begins. Ama Yangjin goes off in the gentle rain to milk her naks and zoms. Finally retreating indoors as the rain pours down, we repeat last night's routine of tea, potatoes and conversation.

The next morning, when I awake, I am alone in the hut. Outside, the sun is bright. Not a cloud can be seen. Except for the vivid green of the near hillsides, this could be a day in the dry, clear winter. Although I have a long day's walk ahead of me, I linger.

Soon Ama Yangjin threads her way through the wildflowers to the doorstep of the hut. "Don't forget," she says: "Walk early in the morning, before it rains!"

WINTER PILGRIMAGE

Norbu fingers his prayer beads as we shuffle along with the crowd in the dim afternoon light. Even in Kathmandu, the January afternoon is chilly; reminding me of how cold it must be now in the mountains. It is no wonder that people from the Himalaya leave their mountain homes to come to the lowlands on pilgrimage and to escape the intense cold.

Norbu leads the way as his wife and I follow him in the crowd circling the great white monument. The momentum of the crowd is like being in a river. To move upstream against the current would be impossible.

The walk around the monument is one continuous corner. Like a river rising in a rainstorm, the mass of people circling the monument grows with the lengthening shadows. The soft light of the setting sun glitters on the gilded spire.

The great monument is a stupa, which represents the Buddha. The spire, with its thirteen rings, symbolizes the spiritual development of the Buddha. Stupas in Nepal have a square base under the spire. The eyes painted on each side of the square represent the wisdom and insight that come with spiritual development.

"I come every winter for a few weeks to pay homage to this great place," says Norbu. He is not alone. Buddhist people from the length of the Himalaya have travelled days and weeks to visit this pilgrimage place.

Most other pilgrimage places that Himalayan Buddhists visit in the winter were important sites in the life of the historical Shakyamuni Buddha about 2,500 years ago.

The great stupa of Bouddha is an exception. Its history relates directly to the establishment of Buddhism in Tibet about 1,200 years ago. It is the largest stupa in Nepal and all of South Asia. A huge white dome, it sits in the middle of the Kathmandu valley like the jewel in a lotus or the centre of a mandala.

The Bouddha stupa in Kathmandu is a popular pilgrimage site.

Butter lamps are lit as offerings.

The devout keep track of their mantras on prayer beads.

"We have a story about the building of the stupa a thousand years ago.

"A poor poultry woman had four sons whom she supported by working hard. Eventually, she saved enough money to approach the king of the valley to ask for enough land upon which to build a monument to the previous Buddha, the Amitaba Buddha. The king rejected her request but the woman kept trying.

"Finally the king granted her as much land as could be covered by one water buffalo hide. The woman cut the hide into strips and sewed them together end to end. When she spread out the strips, they circled this large area.

"The woman and her four sons commenced work on their massive undertaking — hauling earth and stones. After two years, the woman passed away. Her sons completed the stupa after another two years. At the dedication ceremony of the great stupa, the crowds saw rainbow clouds in the sky. It was a very auspicious omen.

"Eventually the sons were reborn as the four men who worked together to establish Buddhism in Tibet and found its first monastery. As Guru Rinpoche, the King of Tibet and the monastery abbot and teacher, they worked just as they had previously on the stupa. So we see Bouddha as the place from which our religion first started."

The story explains why Bouddha draws thousands of Tibetan Buddhist pilgrims each winter. It has been a hub of Himalayan Buddhism in Nepal for decades. Thousands of refugees from Tibet have settled here, and many Tibetan-style monasteries have sprung out of the rice paddy fields.

The population swells each winter as pilgrims arrive from the mountains. They crowd into homes, sleeping on the floors of relatives' homes or in tents on the grounds of monasteries.

Norbu and his wife are staying at their niece's house in Kathmandu. Her house is crowded with relatives from the Khumbu who have come either on pilgrimage or just finished working in the fall trekking season.

"This old man is ready to go home," says a voice behind me as Norbu and his wife reappear beside me.

"If you've finished, let's share a taxi back into the city."

Stepping through the archway over the entrance to the stupa compound is like moving from a quiet river to a storm at sea. Taxis, people and buses moved in random directions.

Norbu and his wife smile as they just keep on fingering their prayer beads.

Zurra, the protector deity of the sacred valleys around Khumbu

Part Four

CEREMONY AND CELEBRATION

A CELEBRATION OF COMMUNITY SPIRIT

This is the best time of year," says Dolma. "Everyone comes home to their village at this time, even if they stay in Kathmandu."

The year revolves around this festival of *Dumchi*, unique to the Sherpas. Each village in Khumbu celebrates Dumchi, which usually falls in late June or early July. It is the start of the summer monsoon. People have just finished planting crops, and many will soon take their livestock to the high pastures for three months. Now, Dumchi also coincides with the return of many Sherpas from work on treks and expeditions.

The high-pitched wail of *gyalling*, a pair of horns, urges us up the hill to where a crowd has gathered in the village gonda. Two Tengboche monks came to Nauche several days before to help with the preparations for the festival.

Ninety years ago, village men with religious training would perform the rituals. Now, the village gonda invites monks from local monasteries to lead the Dumchi prayers. Tengboche Rinpoche comes for six days to officiate at the Dumchi ceremonies.

Dolma's brother, Dorje, finds us in the crowd. He wears a long woollen *chuba* and a grey hat. We follow him down a short, winding track between steeply terraced potato fields.

Prayers to the Khumbu protector deity at the start of Dumchi

Dorje explains, "It's our turn this year to be one of the eight *Dumchi lawas*, the festival sponsors," as Dolma counts several thousand rupees into her brother's hand. He carefully records the amount in his notebook. When Dolma's turn as Dumchi lawa comes, he and anyone else she has helped in previous years will reciprocate.

Each year, eight families have a turn as a Dumchi lawa, who must provide one dinner and one lunch to all the villagers gathered in the community gonda. Tomorrow, the first day of the festival, is Dorje's turn to serve dinner. His wife supervises an assembly-line production. Several relatives and friends help prepare as much food as possible today, before they carry it up to cook in the gonda kitchen. Dolma sits down, picks up a spare knife and starts slicing potatoes.

Monks come from Tengboche for the Dumchi in Nauche.

"Tomorrow will be a busy day," says Dorje. "Besides giving everyone dinner, I must participate in deity-appeasing rituals to put up the prayer flags at the big boulders above the town."

The next morning, Dolma's husband, Sherap, has been busy preparing prayer flags. Dressed in his dark grey chuba and hat, Sherap places the flags outside the house.

Khumbila, the protector deity of Khumbu, is honoured on this second day of Dumchi. All the men of the village are going up the hillside to a huge boulder on which is carved and painted an image of Guru Rinpoche. Although only the men of the village attend this ceremony, Sherap invites me to join him on the hillside. As I follow Sherap up the steep mountainside, I wonder why

Sharing chang for good fortune

the women are excluded; the only other Sherpa ritual that is exclusively for men is the worship of protector deities in the gondas.

All the men of the village have gathered at the boulder, wearing traditional woollen robes and hats. Three monks and the eight Dumchi lawas are already here reciting prayers. Four men clamber about the boulders to place a new string of prayer flags. As each man arrives, he takes his bamboo sticks with the prayer flags to the base of the boulder and places these colourful offerings into a cairn of rocks.

Smearing tsampa on the face while saying "May you live to have a white beard!"

After the puja is over, everyone shares *chang* (rice or millet beer) brought in brass-trimmed wooden flasks. Once the drinking is over, everyone shares best wishes for a long life by smearing a handful of tsampa, barley flour, over each other's faces. I jump as someone comes up behind me and spreads a handful of tsampa over my face. Everyone is laughing. However this custom originated, the laughter it generates is sure to dissolve any existing tensions between villagers.

A line forms on the edge of the wide trail. Sherpa folk dancing begins, accompanied by three traditional folk songs. The singing ends with a mighty "*Lha, Gyalo!* [Gods are victorious]" and everyone tosses a fistful of tsampa in the air.

Traditional Sherpa line dancing at the end of the protector puja

The first to leave is a ninety-year-old elder who has actively participated in the dancing and ritual. He wears a gold-coloured silk robe with a raw silk sash over his shoulder. On his head is a stiff woollen tam. He sings and smiles as he leads the line down the path to the village. The crowd shuffles and staggers back to the village, singing all the way, and everyone goes home to sleep off the effects of the chang.

Later, in the afternoon, dressed in their best clothes, people head up to the gonda on the hill. Several women wear their gold charm boxes encrusted with turquoise and gems, called *gau*. Other women wear necklaces of coral, amber and black-and-white *dzi* (an agate-like stone). Everyone gathers in the courtyard of the village gonda, with the men and women sitting on opposite sides of the stone-paved courtyard.

Flute music announces the entry of Tengboche Rinpoche and other senior monks. They take seats on a platform along the back wall of the courtyard. During some prayers, a village elder

Traditional Sherpa garb

fulfills the role of the custodian of the village rituals. He reads from a long scroll, in very traditional, old-fashioned language, the history and rules relating to the Dumchi festival.

The tradition of Dumchi was started in Pangboche about 350 years ago to gather the villagers together in the spirit of religious and community duty. Apparently, Dumchi-type prayers are also recited in Tibet, but rice and food are offered only in Khumbu.

The Sherpas seem to be unique for their community spirit as they strive to maintain harmony among themselves and with the world around them. Giving and receiving are ritualized in daily life, in religion and at celebrations such as Dumchi.

The festival sponsors feed the entire village.

Tengboche Rinpoche has described to me how an early village leader and priest, Lama Sangwa Dorje, saw a need to unite the early settlers in Khumbu.

At first, everyone went to gondas in Pangboche, Thame or Rimijung. Later, as the population grew, people established gondas in Khumjung, Nauche and Phortse, where Dumchi could be celebrated. Each village knows celebrates Dumchi in its own unique style — but in every Dumchi festival, families take turns to sponsor the festival and provide food and drinks.

Finally, Dorje and his friends and relatives bring out huge pots of rice, potato and meat curry and yogourt to the centre of the courtyard. Dolma and several women ladle it out on plates while

Dorje and several relatives serve the food. Feeding the entire village takes less than an hour. Dorje and his family quickly gather the dirty plates and remove the empty pots.

The next evening, another family of Dumchi sponsors have their turn to feed the village. After the feast, everyone stays for the ritual exorcism of negative energy from the village. Rinpoche and the monks recite prayers as a slow, steady chant.

Flutes announce the entrance of a dancer representing Zurra, the protective deity of the hidden, sacred valley of Khembalung and the valleys around it, including Khumbu. Zurra circles and spins in the courtyard, which minutes earlier was a dining room.

After Zurra returns into the gonda, the long horns bellow their long, deep drone. Kids crowd around the two young monks playing the horns, who are only a couple of years older.

A majestic masked figure enters the courtyard. Dorje Trolo is the wrathful form of Guru Rinpoche. His steps are slow, vigilant. He takes a seat so the Dumchi lawas can tie khatas on the mask and bow to this fierce protector.

A Dumchi lawa carefully lays firewood on a platform prepared earlier by the monks. He places a wok full of butter on the firewood.

The courtyard is quiet but packed with several hundred people anticipating the next event. Into the silence burst two powerful figures.

Two monks in the colourful robes and black hats of magicians circle the courtyard. They represent, or perhaps become, the traditional priests skilled in the methods of manipulating the forces of nature. Each gesture implies power. Each stretch of their arms speaks of their determination to overcome any negative forces accumulated over the past year.

Tengboche Rinpoche descends from his throne and stands at the edge of the open space wearing the red hat modelled after Guru Rinpoche's, worn by all those skilled in the use of mystical powers. His prayers, read from a text held by a young monk standing next to him, are slow and solemn. He glances at a paper suspended by a string over the fire preparations.

The Black Hat dancer promotes spiritual power.

The paper is a vessel for the negative energy being coaxed into that paper by the prayers. The fire is lit. As the butter melts, scoops of liquor are added to the wok. Suddenly the butter boils over, sending a tower of flames thirty feet into the night sky.

The crowd where I stand is pressed back four feet from its original position. A collective sigh escapes from the audience. The Black Hat magicians dance a finale. Rinpoche goes into the gonda and the villagers file home.

Dolma appears at my side. "Tonight was good. Once, the flames didn't go very high. Maybe it was an omen. Nobody knew." Sherap seems uncomfortable at her telling me this, perhaps unsure of how I, as a foreigner, might perceive this "superstition."

Again the next night, everyone gathers in the gonda courtyard. Two more lawa families feed everyone.

Destroying the negative energy of the past year

A large effigy and some small figures stand on a table in the centre of the courtyard. People use a handful of tsampa left from making the effigy to rub their arms and legs as a ritual purification. They leave the tsampa in a basket.

The Black Hat dancers deposit one of the figures in a hole under the flagstones of the courtyard. They carry the larger effigy and basket of tsampa from the courtyard and burn them in a massive bonfire of old baskets.

On the final night, the villagers dress in their best clothes to gather one last time. Silk and jewellery shimmer in the lantern light, generating a truly festive atmosphere.

After days of ritual purification, today, the last day of Dumchi, the villagers will receive a blessing from Tengboche Rinpoche. Tonight's lawas and their helpers once again distribute food.

To the urging of flutes and horns, the Rinpoche and the monks commence reading prayers. One of the monks, Thubten, walks through the audience spooning out tiny portions of blessed nectar in the palms of the villagers' outstretched hands. The nectar is swallowed quickly. Next, Thubten dispenses a few uncooked rice grains to everyone. After a crescendo in the chanting and horns, everyone tosses their rice grains as a final offering. Finally, the Dumchi lawas and their families

Dispensing a few uncooked rice grains to everyone

The festival sponsors for the coming year receive tormas during the last ritual.

approach the stage to receive their blessings. Though orderly at first, the line quickly becomes a gently jostling mass of people.

After the blessing ceremony is over and people have returned to their seats, the Rinpoche and the monks go inside the gonda. Meanwhile, as all of this year's Dumchi lawas come forward and stand in line in the middle of the courtyard, the custodian of the village rituals reads a list of names. Those named also approach the courtyard.

Khatas are draped around their necks and each man is presented with a *torma*, a dough-and-butter sculpture representing the passing on of the Dumchi obligations to them. There is much laughter and chatter as each of this year's outgoing Dumchi lawas pass a wide brass bowl filled to the brim with chang down the line of new lawas. Each family will keep the torma on their shrine for the next year.

Later I ask Sherap how he feels about being chosen as a Dumchi lawa for next year, with its incredible expense and responsibility. Sherap replies that as a new family, he and his wife are proud to have been chosen as lawas. It means that they are now recognized as an independent family and as full members of the community.

Meanwhile, as the official ceremonies end, a party evolves. As people link arms behind their backs, a line forms. Singing a lilting melody, the dancers keep the beat with an intricate series of steps of Sherpa folk dances.

Sherap says, "Right now, some of us have other things to do. Someone has to look after his trekking company in Kathmandu; another has a chance to go to Switzerland; but we give up all that for a while to come here together.

"We pray together, we dance together and we eat together. What is important now, at Dumchi, is that we are all here cooperating together."

"For the Good of the Whole World"

In his kitchen at Tengboche, Pasang Thondrup, Tengboche Rinpoche's younger brother, talks about the coming *Mani Rimdu* festival. Every year hundreds of people come to this colourful festival here at the monastery.

"We call the masked dances *chaam*. They are only a small part of Mani Rimdu," Pasang explains. Mani Rimdu combines religious ritual with pageantry and entertainment. Sherpas from several villages come to receive a blessing, while foreign travellers come to see the colourful masked dances. For the abbot and monks, the three days of public events celebrate the completion of ten days of non-stop prayers.

At Tengboche monastery, the monks perform Mani Rimdu each year in the ninth month of the Tibetan lunar calendar, which usually falls on the full moon of November. Other monasteries in Solu-Khumbu celebrate this ritual at different times: for instance, Thame, which does it in the fourth month. Tengboche draws the largest audience because it is on the trekking route to Mount Everest and, by coincidence, the festival occurs during the trekking season.

Pasang, who was once a monk, explains, "Mani Rimdu was first celebrated here to consecrate the monastery when it opened in 1919." He left the monastery twenty years ago but is still a reliable source of information on Sherpa culture.

He continues, "Though Mani Rimdu only began here in 1919, the dancing, called chaam, is a tradition in many different Buddhist celebrations. Chaam originated over a thousand years ago when Guru Rinpoche blessed Tibet's first monastery by imitating his favourite god. In this dance, the god became one with him. Chaam is performed in monastery rituals and other important Sherpa festivals.

"The name of this festival: *mani* is the prayers to the god of compassion, going on in the gonda right now; *ril* is the little dough pellets — the long-life pills distributed in the blessing ceremony; and *dup* is the blessing on the pellets."

Tengboche Rinpoche in outdoor ritual

Preparing the sand mandala

Later, inside the gonda, a kerosene lantern illuminates fresco-covered walls. A painting of the god embodying compassion, *Phawa Chyenrezig*, has eleven heads and a thousand arms that enable him to act for the good of the whole world. The monks direct these prayers to this deity and invoke blessings into a tray of "long-life pills."

Chiwong Dorje, the prayer leader, sits at the head of the row of monks. Like a conductor, he manages the symphony of voices and instruments, keeping the beat by tapping his cymbals, an instrument played by the most experienced monks.

At a pause in the chanting, the gonda custodian, Ngawang, shows me a large table surrounded by silk curtains in the centre of the room.

A multi-coloured sand mandala covers the tabletop. This delicate and complex piece of art depicts squares and concentric rings representing the development of an enlightened mind. For four days, four monks created the mandala grain by grain. Each grain of sand augments the merit generated during the mandala's creation. In Mani Rimdu's final ritual, the monks destroy the mandala to symbolize the impermanence of our "real" outside world.

The next morning, the monastery grounds are crowded with villagers, yaks and trekkers. Tourists wearing bright-coloured parkas stand next to Sherpa women dressed in woollen robes, striped aprons and gold jewellery. Merchants sell trinkets and clothing, from blankets on the ground. Monks take advantage of a pause in the rituals to survey the scene.

Eventually, a procession of monks emerges from the gonda. They take seats on a small stage or benches. At the far end sit nuns and wealthy Sherpa sponsors, who present the abbot with financial contributions for the monastery. Other villagers also distribute cash to each monk and ani present.

Several Sherpa families offer tea and more tea.

The monks recite the final prayers over the "long-life" pills. According to Rinpoche, "This is a *tshe-wang*, a life-empowerment ceremony. Long life and good fortune enable one to generate more merit through good actions."

As high-pitched flutes start wailing, villagers surge forward to receive the blessings. Eventually, I join the line and pull a khata out of my pocket to place on the pile by Rinpoche. As I bow, he touches his ritual vase to my head in blessing.

A round, older monk beams as he places a pill in my cupped hands. Each monk along the long, low table adds a spoonful of *tshe-chang* (nectar) to my palm. Turning from the stage, I swallow everything and copy the correct Sherpa procedure by wiping my hand on top of my head, not wasting a precious, blessed drop.

Tengboche Rinpoche at the start of the blessing ceremony

The drone of long horns signals the end of the ceremony. The monks gather the dishes of leftover long-life pills, don their crested hats and return to the gonda.

At twilight I weave my way across the field, now crowded with trekkers' tents. Inside the hotel, the dining room is packed with trekkers, the kitchen with Sherpas.

Attending the festival at the monastery is an opportunity for Sherpas to visit with friends and relatives from other villages. It is a time for sharing food and drink, laughter and life.

Tengboche Rinpoche at the start of the blessing ceremony

With Sherpa etiquette, a young man offers chang to everyone in the kitchen, filling each glass to the brim and insisting they take three sips. Then he refills the glass. When he comes to me, I politely refuse. Suddenly, Pasang's wife holds the glass to my lips to force me to drink. I eventually give in, taking three sips of chang, while wondering why such gentle people are so assertive in their hospitality.

Gradually, everyone wanders to the gonda courtyard. Arms linked behind their backs, a circle of Sherpas fills the courtyard. Men dance in one half of the line, women in the other. As the lilting sound of their folk songs fills the courtyard, three monks roll in a large plastic barrel. Another monk carries a massive armful of khatas. The monks offer a large wooden bowl full of chang to the first, eldest Sherpa in the line, who takes three sips and bows to accept a khata around his neck. The dancing continues undisturbed as each person receives a khata and three sips of chang.

Pasang comes up beside me. "This is a thank you from the monastery," he says, "for attending the festival, dancing and helping to make it a success. This creates some merit … for the good of all the Sherpas, for all of Nepal. It's for the good of the whole world."

DANCE OF THE GODS

In the courtyard the next morning, a single masked monk emerges from the gonda. As he spreads his arms, his slow, measured pace matches the drone of the long horns. Then the clashing of cymbals changes the tempo — he leaps and turns.

After half an hour, the monk is visibly breathing hard. Once, I asked a monk how he could see through the small holes in the mask's nostrils. "When we put on the masks, we become the gods," he replied, "so we don't need to see."

Rinpoche explains: "To perform a chaam, the monk must meditate and practise. Certain movements, sounds, aromas and sights can awaken our psyche and stimulate our awareness. The chaam are a meditation that reveals the gods within us. The portrayal of these gods by the dancers generates merit for everyone."

Rinpoche and senior monks sit in a balcony chanting the specific prayers for each chaam. At the sound of conch shells, the lone figure retreats into the gonda.

Several dancers appear, wearing wide-brimmed black hats. According to Rinpoche, this chaam invokes a state of mind to improve one's life, longevity, appearance, health, intelligence and ability to fight bad spirits. The chaam provides spiritual power.

These dignified dancer-magicians carry daggers to destroy a symbol of evil, a floppy doll. The dance ends with skeletons entering briefly to gleefully throw the doll in the air and scamper away.

For several minutes, the crowd eagerly awaits the next performance, until a stooped figure appears on the gonda steps. Everyone howls with laughter at Mi-Tsering, the "long-life man" wearing a mask of an aged man with bushy eyebrows, a long grey beard and a huge smile.

For the next hour, Mi-Tsering gently pokes fun at the folly of being overly pious. He finds a good-natured foreigner to act as his "student" and stooge. The pious old man teaches all the proper rituals using all the wrong methods. The stooge gets flour thrown in his face as Mi-Tsering

Gonpa (Maha-kala), a protector of Buddhism

instructs him to make offerings. The chuckling continues as Mi-Tsering hobbles from the courtyard.

The deep bass horns resume. Eight gods gather on the gonda steps. Each executes a swirling, turning solo dance around the courtyard, and then all eight figures dance together.

A sweetly smiling white mask represents Tseringma, the eldest long-life sister-goddess. Gonpa (Maha-kala), a powerful protector of Buddhism, wears a dark blue mask with a fierce scowl, bulging eyes and flaring eyebrows.

Chyenrezig, or Mahadeva, the great god personifying compassion in action, wears a red, smiling mask with a third eye representing awareness. The gods twirl and turn, twirl and turn, then retreat into the gonda.

Anticipation fills the air.

Soon an outrageous figure, named

The "long-life man" pokes fun at being overly pious.

Thogden, swaggers into the sacred space. He talks constantly, impersonating an Indian holy man.

Despite the chilly air, Thogden wears only a thin cotton robe, but tells the audience what fools they are to sit in the cold. He claims he will prove his holiness and teach them the proper ways of practising religion.

A fierce representation of Guru Rinpoche

Actually, he uses humour to present subtle religious messages by mocking everything the Sherpas revere.

An assistant creeps into the courtyard wearing a monkey mask and an old black robe. Thogden jumps him. The pair rolls across the courtyard. When the assistant escapes, Thogden takes flying leaps at the audience as he tries to catch him.

Finally, they sit cross-legged on the ground before a low table. Thogden teaches his assistant to prepare offerings. He fumbles. Flour flies in the air. Thogden's dialogue gains momentum. Laughter consumes the audience.

Tseringma, eldest of the long-life sister deities

Thogden holds up an object wrapped in silk. He runs up to the crowd and blesses people by touching this sacred object on their heads. Thogden shrieks. He removes the silk wrapping and displays a toy bear. Thogden pulls its cord and the bear plays a lullaby. The crowd squirms with mirth.

Thogden rummages in his bag. He rises holding another silk-wrapped object. He repeats his previous routine, except this time many more people bow their heads to receive the blessing.

Chyenrezig, a deity personifying compassion

Thogden stops and jumps around the courtyard, holding the object high while screaming that the audience are fools. Once again he unwraps the silk covering — to display a dirty old shoe — and asks the audience why they chased after any blessing. The people respond by laughing even more.

The crowds of Sherpas enjoy the comic events.

Friends enjoying the festival

After an hour of improvised comedy, Thogden demonstrates his spiritual strength by bending his body over a long metal sword for his finale. The atmosphere changes; the audience is silent in suspense. The sword is real and the monk requires considerable agility to avoid stabbing himself.

A lone khata floats down to the performer; others follow. Money wrapped in khatas floats down around Thogden. Suddenly, he leans his whole weight upon the sword. The crowd gasps as he jerks to the side and the sword clatters on the flagstones. Thogden dashes into the gonda while two young monks gather the khatas and props.

As dusk falls, monks bring in kerosene lanterns. Once again the Black Hat dancers circle and swirl through the sacred space of the courtyard. Their shadows dance over the audience.

Light reflects off a lone dancer's swirling silk robe. The monk wears the black hat and costume of a priest. His gestures and movements suggest strength and spiritual power. The intensity of the dancer's concentration captivates the audience. He turns toward me but is looking beyond.

His gestures drive evil from the courtyard, from the monastery, from the world. He clears a sacred space for the dance of the gods, the hidden gods of wisdom and compassion present within everyone.

Note: In 2001 the Sherpa manager of a conservation project in Tibet took monks from Khumbu to instruct the Rongbuk monks on the Mani Rimdu chaam, which was being revived at Rongbuk monastery.

Dehu Rinpoche in 1987

Part Five

THE WHEEL OF LIFE

FUNERALS ... PASSAGES

"When you die, what do you take with you? Your money, your house, even your wife and family do not go with you through the afterlife to your next lifetime.

"But your spiritual and mental accomplishments ... are what the mind takes with it to its next physical body."

Tengboche Rinpoche's words return as I sit on the mountainside at Tengboche watching preparations for a cremation.

Family and friends regard the timing as fortunate because the deceased woman was in a very happy state of mind, having just received a blessing at the monastery.

Sherpas say that terrifying, accidental deaths are a bad way to die, because the mind is in a state of turmoil and there is no opportunity to balance one's thoughts. Mental and emotional states are believed to affect one's afterlife and rebirth. Lamas encourage a dying person to meditate through the transition from life to death.

On this third day after her death, the woman's body is being cremated at Tengboche. Several loads of firewood are arranged in a square log-cabin formation about three feet high. Cremation sites are usually located on a ridgetop in an airy place close to the sky. Seven monks say prayers on the side.

A cremation pyre and monks saying prayers at funeral of ordinary person

A few male relatives wash and prepare the body behind a blanket held out as a screen. They anoint the eyes, mouth and top of the head with butter and place the body sitting cross-legged inside the box of firewood. As they close the top with more wood, the family members tie khatas to the wood. One last farewell.

The fire is lit and smoke billows into the blue sky. The family offers tea and cookies to everyone present. It takes several hours to complete the cremation. Fragments of the heavy bones in the hips and skull that did not burn totally in the fire are collected and disposed of carefully.

Some bone shards are kept to be blessed by a lama and ground into powder, which is mixed with clay and pressed into base relief moulds of Buddha images. The family keeps these relics until the 49th day after the death and then takes them to mountain caves or monuments, *chhur-ung*, especially built to store the clay images.

In the meantime, they prepare for the main funeral prayers, called *Shi-Tu*, which, depending on the finances of the family, last from three to fifteen days in the home of the deceased or a close relative. A few days later, several monks and village lamas are reciting the prayers in the main room of the family home. Several family members help prepare food for everyone.

On this second-last day of prayers, a measure of rice grains is given to anyone who comes to the house. Late in the afternoon, monks blow conch shells as a summons. Villagers queue to receive a measure of grain.

The nephew instructs me, "You must receive measures of rice and tsampa. Our family's generosity at this time helps earn merit for a good rebirth for my aunt's spirit."

Giving and receiving are important ways of generating merit. Purely intended generosity during the rituals gains merit for the future, so it is important to receive the hospitality graciously so that the giver may earn merit.

The funerals bridge the everyday and the metaphysical — meeting practical emotional needs while serving spiritual requirements.

The funeral rites in the home are a catharsis to meet the emotional need of acknowledging the loss. As the rituals end for the day, the nephew says, "After one year, we'll do another puja for my aunt's spirit in its new life."

AFTER AN ACCOMPLISHED LIFETIME...

Over 700 people have come for this special occasion on the mountainside above Pangboche. A highly respected lama, Dehu Rinpoche, is being cremated.

There is a mixture of reactions — solemn and intense at times, then suddenly joyous when several people start pointing to the clouds and whispering.

Dehu Rinpoche and nuns in 1987

A shaft of light comes through the clouds. It has not been raining, yet the light creates a long beam of multiple rainbows but not in an arch like normal rainbows. The phenomenon lasts for several minutes and then dissolves.

Dehu Rinpoche was known for his spiritual accomplishments, healing using herbal medicine, and religious teaching and advice. He did years of meditation retreats in caves in the mountains.

More recently, he had started a Buddhist school for girls at his small nunnery in a spectacular location at the base of a cliff.

Dehu Rinpoche passed away in August 1989 at the age of 86. He was meditating at the time, so, like many high lamas, his body maintained the cross-legged position for several days after the death as one consequence of his spiritual accomplishments.

"*Sem*," says Tengboche Rinpoche, "is our word for the mind or spirit. It is indestructible. We learn to manage and control our Sem in meditation and certain rituals.

"After death, the Sem leaves the body but still exists. As a person is dying, the family or attendants call a lama to use prayers to ease the Sem out of the body via the head.

"If the spirit leaves by other passages, it may have difficulty in the future. After exiting by the eyes or nose, it may be animal or human. Departures via the head may lead to higher existences. The lama doing this ritual must be well qualified and experienced."

During this time immediately after the death, lamas and monks sit with the body, reading the prayers and giving instructions to the spirit on which path to follow in the afterlife transition period, the *phardo*.

For an accomplished Buddhist practitioner like Dehu Rinpoche, the body is preserved in salt to allow the mind, body and spirit to stay together through the phardo.

When it is time for the cremation, his body is then wrapped in silks and ceremonial robes and carried in a sedan to the cremation site high on a mountainside.

Many of the prayers and rituals are similar to those for ordinary people, but the cremation is very special. A rock and mud plaster crematorium has been constructed especially for Dehu Rinpoche's cremation.

An attendant gently places the body inside the crematorium and sets special offerings in with the body. Finally, he fills the entrance with more firewood. Sherpas file past to offer one last khata to Dehu Rinpoche.

Tengboche Rinpoche and the monks offer prayers as the attending monk ignites the crematorium and many people present commence the ritual of creating merit by doing circumambulations of the site.

Hundreds of people attended Dehu Rinpoche's cremation.

Smoke billows and swirls from the crematorium. It glances off the small Buddha placed on the top of the crematorium.

Later, for both lamas and lay people, the Shi-Tu prayers may be done to reconcile the calm aspects of the deceased's mind with the fierce. Tengboche Rinpoche describes these prayers:

"The purpose of the Shi-Tu is to purify and gain merit for the person's spirit.

"Our minds are not stable, because we see things as good and bad. These desires and dislikes are like dirt on a window. Through prayer, meditation, Shi-Tu and trying to keep a balance in our thoughts, we can clear our minds so that we can perceive ourselves more clearly."

A tiny Buddha statue atop a crematorium

As people circle the crematorium, someone sees the rainbow clouds. Soon everyone is watching. The mood becomes joyous. These rainbow-like apparitions in the sky are apparently an auspicious sign for the rebirth of the lama.

After a few hours, the smoke dissipates and people drift down to the nunnery, where the nuns feed them a lunch of rice and stew. Later in the day, the community holds a meeting. The main speaker teases people into promising significant sums of money to raise funds for the nuns, who would otherwise be destitute without the offerings that always came to Dehu Rinpoche for his sound advice and wisdom, a result of his mental and spiritual accomplishments of a lifetime.

New mothers are fed ample nutritious food, such as eggs and meat.

Birth ... Rebirth

"My baby might come just before the monsoon." My friend is just starting to show in her unreveal-ing Sherpa dress. She cuddles her three-year-old son as she talks.

"We usually don't talk about our pregnancies and when the baby is due." She elaborates, "When the baby comes, our energy can be low for a few days. It can make a woman vulnerable. Many people lose babies during pregnancy."

Until thirty years ago, iodine deficiency caused serious problems. Tibetan rock salt, still favoured for its flavour over sea salt from India, lacks iodine, as does the normal diet in these mountain regions. A few old people had massive goitres. Others were born mentally handicapped or deaf because their mothers were iodine-deficient. Women often had several pregnancies that ended with stillborn babies or infants dying. After women received an iodine injection, they usu-ally had normal pregnancies and healthy children.

Recently, a woman had two stillborn babies and one that died after a month. The doctor at the hospital in Khunde, established by Sir Edmund Hillary's Himalayan Trust, figured out that the woman had an iodine deficiency, which was causing the problems with childbearing.

My friend continues, "I haven't decided whether to go to the hospital again. This *phujung* [son] was born there, but it would be nice to have the baby here at home, with my sister and friends helping. I have to either go early and wait at the hospital, or hope that I can walk there once the pains start.

"At home we can do everything that we believe helps the baby come faster and easier. We like to keep warm, so we put on lots of clothes and drink cups and cups of tea. Also, we like to sit or squat, which is more comfortable.

"Our mother, or whoever is helping, gives us a blessing with a little smudge of butter on our foreheads. As soon as possible after the birth, we have eggs and a glass of chang. We eat as much as we can after the baby is born, especially meat and eggs. We need that good food for our baby and ourselves to be strong.

"Most Sherpa women do not drink alcohol, but we have a special chang drink for after the delivery to help our milk come. First, we melt butter in a pan with some fennel seeds. Then, we beat an egg in with the butter. Last, we pour in chang and mix it well," she explains.

"Delivery chang" is usually served in a soup bowl, from which this tasty drink is slowly sipped. I know a few families where delivery chang was a favourite winter drink, whatever the occasion.

"I fed milk to this one until he was about two years old, but when he was four or five weeks old we started feeding him porridge of butter and tsampa. He was such a hungry tiger! He still is!"

The little boy devours a large bowl of stew. I remember his naming ceremony three years before. Several people had already gathered in the family's home. Khonjo Chombi and another village lama recited prayers and tossed rice grains in the air as offerings petitioning good fortune for the child.

Finally, Khonjo Chombi rose from his seat and pulled a parchment with the name from under the khata that secured it to the main pillar of the house. With a flourish, he opened the folded paper and recited a brief prayer. He cleared his throat and announced "Nima Wangyal."

Nima means Sunday. About two-thirds of Sherpas are named for the day of the week on which they were born. Nima is followed by Dawa, Mingma, Lhakpa, Phurba, Pasang and Pemba. Wangyal means powerful one. The second name usually has religious or auspicious symbolism.

The new father and his friends tied a slender young tree decorated with khatas next to the outside door of the house. More khatas followed as everyone gave a khata to the mother, father and child and tied one to the main pillar of the house.

Khatas are essential in the rituals of the wheel of life — for birth, marriages and death. They are presented in an extraordinary variety of situations, including when one visits one's elders or a lama, pays homage to a religious figure or site, passes through an auspicious place or expresses good luck, farewell or thanks.

As the naming ceremony became a party, arriving neighbours were served several rounds of chang, tea and food. Giving and receiving would continue the rest of the night.

DISCOVERY OF A REINCARNATE LAMA

"The reincarnate of Gomchen Khambala Lama has been found," says Tengboche Rinpoche. For days, I have been hearing stories about a young boy being discovered as a reincarnate lama who lived for many years in a hermitage above Lukla.

I remember the day the Lama passed away years before. On my way down to Lukla to fly to Kathmandu, a gale force wind began at about 3 a.m. It howled, spun dust and tore the roof off the newly completed cultural centre. At the same time the next morning, the wind stopped as mysteriously as it had begun.

Sherpas I met along the trail attributed the wind to the lama's passing. Now, five years later, I hear that the lama's reincarnation has been found.

"The boy is in Pangboche. Visit his parents while you are there."

Upon my arrival in Pangboche, a stone flies past as I round a bend in the trail. I look up just in time to see a small boy disappear into the shrubbery. This apparently is him.

"Namaste," the father greets me at his kitchen door, "come in, have a seat. Have you been hearing stories about one of my children?

"Apparently, the Tibetan herbal doctor Dehu Rinpoche was visited in his dreams by Lama Gomchen-la. The next morning the Rinpoche said, 'The child who comes today is the reincarnate of Lama Gomchen-la.'

"My son was a year old and suddenly very sick. That day, my wife took him to see Dehu Rinpoche. He told her that our child would be fine and not to worry.

"Then, last year, two Sherpa elders came to visit. One started pulling at his beard with an old pair of tweezers. My son jumped up and shouted at him, 'Those are my tweezers!' The other leaned forward and handed my son brand new shiny tweezers. 'Perhaps these are your tweezers?'

"My son said, 'No, no, those are not my tweezers. These are my tweezers,' pointing at the old tweezers in the elder's hand. That was last August.

"In November they brought a box carried on a yak. On the trail up to our village gonda, my son saw the box. He went running after them shouting, 'That is my box, give me my box.' The yak driver said it was a tourist's box. My son insisted, 'No, this is my box.' Eventually, they got the box up to the gonda.

"In the morning, they told us to bring our son to the gonda. He identified every object in the box. Then, he told them, 'My mask is not here, please bring my mask.' It was a special mask from Tibet. The elders went back to the lama's hermitage. There in a corner was the mask.

"So, my son was officially recognized as the reincarnate of Gomchen Khambala Lama. We will probably send him to the big monastery in the Solu valley. We may take him to Kathmandu in January and talk to some lamas to decide. It is hard to say; now, he is just a little boy, only four years old. He is always playing.

"Sometimes he says he wants to be a lama. If I give him a *dhamaru*, he plays as he is doing a ritual, but maybe just because he has seen the monks doing it. Now Tengboche Rinpoche has given our son the title Lama Tsewang."

In Sherpa beliefs, all beings pass through lifetimes. Those who achieve a high level of spiritual development are believed to carry the accomplishments of their mind from one lifetime to another.

Of these, the Dalai Lama is the most well known, but he is one of thousands of reincarnate lamas among Himalayan people, including Tengboche, Thame and Dehu rinpoches in Khumbu.

A year later, at Mani Rimdu, Sherpa elders present khatas to respected monks and lamas sitting in a row. The little reincarnate of Gomchen-la Lama sits among them and seems to know the proper procedures.

The blessing ceremony draws to a close. Two monks play a reedy serenade on the high-pitched flutes to signal the completion of the ceremony.

Although he is now a high lama, Tsering Dorje fumbles inside his robes and pulls out a cardboard party whistle. As the monks begin to play the horns, he plays his own shrill serenade on the multi-coloured, feather-tipped whistle.

The parents did not know that their son was the reincarnation of a high lama.

THE WEDDING

"When is Nima finally getting married?"

"Not until she has a second child," responds her father. Traditionally, Sherpas only complete the series of marriage ceremonies after one or two children are born.

"Besides, right now we cannot afford to lose her."

Nima is the chief cook in the family's trekking hotel. While she hustles preparing food for trekkers, other family members tend to and amuse the baby. By having her first children in her family home, Nima has eager relatives ready and willing to provide guidance and support for both delivery and child rearing.

The child's father, Dawa, is a frequent and welcome visitor. Eighteen months before, he suggested to his parents that he and Nima might be a good match. There were many family consultations. This proposal would not just unite two individuals; it would establish ties between two families.

The most significant consultation established that they were from different clans. Marriage within a clan is the strongest prohibition in Sherpa culture. Various Sherpa authorities identify about twenty clans.

The Sherpa word for clan is *ru*, which means "bones." Fathers transmit the bones. Mothers contribute the *sha*, the blood. Marriage with a person of one's mother's clan is permissible if the couple is not related within three generations.

Finally, Dawa's family prepared to request the couple's engagement. They had a village lama perform rituals to beseech a favourable response to their request. They brewed a special batch of chang to present to Nima's family.

Armed with khatas and wooden flasks of chang, Dawa's family delegates visited Nima's parents, who agreed to the proposal. The engagement gave him "visiting rights" to stay with his

The groom and his relatives in procession to the bride's home

fiancée while she remained with her family. Only after the final ceremony would she go to live in the groom's home.

1987. After three years of engagement, Nima has now given birth to two children.

On Nima's wedding day, clashing cymbals start at three in the morning. Today is the most auspicious astrological date for the couple. Village lamas begin the rituals to ensure a successful married life. Meanwhile, Nima is cooking in the kitchen.

Dawa's family is also conducting rituals in their home. Early in the afternoon, his relatives start a procession through the village to Nima's house. Dawa wears an orange silk robe and tasselled hat. One brother holds an umbrella over him as a symbol of protection.

Along the way, neighbours serve chang and tea to Dawa and his relatives. Nima's sister officially greets them, and the village lama leading the procession blesses the chang that she offers them.

Finally, Dawa and his relatives enter the house. They are served a large meal, which they wash down with copious quantities of chang and tea. For the next three days, Nima's relatives take turns entertaining his relatives in their homes.

By the fourth day, Nima has not yet attended any festivities. As she cooks another huge feast for the guests, she assures me that today she will be in the celebrations.

Finally, Nima made her grand entrance into the wedding ceremony. The wedding continued successfully. Nima and her husband had a happy marriage and two more children.

Sadly, after several years, the woman on whom I modelled "Nima" passed away in a sudden illness. Everyone missed her gaiety of spirit. At her husband's request, I have not used the photographs of their wedding.

Kathmandu, 2006.

"Can you go back to your office to check my email," says Sherap as he hurries with preparations for his son's wedding. "I've not had a free moment to see if any friends from overseas are coming for the wedding."

For weeks, both families have worked hard for this final wedding ceremony of their university-educated son and daughter.

This wedding is the first time that all the rituals associated with a traditional Sherpa marriage ceremony are being conducted in Kathmandu. Rather than having the rituals spread over several days, they are all happening on one long day.

After the early-morning procession to the bride's home, the ritual greetings and songs of appreciation have been followed by lunch. Everyone settles into what would have been the fourth day of a traditional wedding in a mountain village.

A respected village elder strides to the centre of the garden. Speaking on behalf of Phurba's family, he greets the groom's entourage:

"This family welcomes you into their home. We realize you have journeyed for many days on difficult tracks over many ridges."

Everyone laughs. This traditional speech recalls the past when marriages were often between couples from distant villages. He ceremonially introduces the families as if they were strangers, although they have been friends for years.

The groom and bride during the marriage rituals

His speech leaves everyone laughing while they wait expectantly.

Phurba enters the garden wearing a heavy silk robe. Tears stream down her face as she sits beside Mingma on a special carpet. In keeping with tradition, she must cry to honour her family, but most brides are emotional at the thought of leaving home and family.

After the lama's blessing, Mingma's father anoints Phurba's forehead with butter while her father anoints Mingma. After the rituals, men from the groom's party blow conch shells and clatter heavy brass cymbals.

They start a wild, swirling dance as Phurba bids farewell to her family. Joining the wild procession, Phurba and Mingma emerge into the lane and get into a heavily decorated car for the short drive to Mingma's house. The dancers lead the procession through the lanes.

Above: The groom's relatives singing their thanks to the bride's family
Left: The groom in traditional clothes

At the gate of Mingma's house, friends offer the procession chang and tea as the couple disembark from the car. Behind them, ten unmarried young women unload Phurba's belongings and inheritance from her parents from another car and prepare to carry it in the procession into her new home.

By Sherpa tradition, sons and daughters inherit their share of family property at their wedding. A woman takes carpets, copper pots, jewellery, clothing, blankets and cash to her new home

Sons usually inherit a share of their parents' immovable property — houses, fields, pastures and livestock. Even now in the city, parents try to build a house for each son or divide an existing house so that each son's family has its own upstairs living space and separate entrance. Sherpas rarely live as extended families. However, the youngest or only son inherits the parents' house and the responsibility to care for them in their old age.

In previous generations, some Sherpas practised the Tibetan tradition of marrying a woman to two or three brothers. This practice prevented the division of the family property into uneconomical units. Offspring of polyandrous marriages refer to their male parents as "big [older] father and little [younger] father." One husband would tend the yak herd while the other was away trading. Despite periodic absences by either husband, one was usually at home with the wife and children.

The practice of polyandry included situations where, if an older brother died, his unmarried younger brother took responsibility for the widow and children. However, for a generation, there have not been any new officially polyandrous marriages among the Sherpas in Khumbu.

For families without sons, the inheritance customs allow the youngest daughter to inherit her family home and marry a man from a family with many sons, who inherits a share of his family's moveable property to take to his wife's house.

By Sherpa custom, friends and relatives contribute to the bride's inheritance. Once her belongings are unloaded and displayed, Phurba's cousin records each gift and its value. Her parents are now indebted to return similar gifts when each contributor's daughter marries.

Phurba now smiles brightly in her new home. As in the village, her husband's relatives will take turns providing feasts for several days.

After five days, she and Mingma will visit her parents' home for a ritual to deposit some good fortune generated by the wedding ceremonies back at her parents' home. Then, she will return to her work as a dentist.

Sherpas place a dab of butter on vessels or bottles of drinks for good luck.

Part Six

EPILOGUE

PRAYER FLAGS OVER TIN ROOFS

2000. "Why do the tourists hate the tin roofs?" asks Tashi. "Do they really think that we should live under a leaky wooden roof to keep our culture?"

Leaving the protection of a tin roof, Ang Maya and I open our umbrellas and step into the rain. Water splashes up our legs as the downpour bounces off the flagstones. The clatter of the heavy rain on the many tin roofs is deafening.

There are so many more new houses in Khumbu. Some external changes are striking. Most houses now have large glass windows. Some hotels even have indoor plumbing. Instead of the basic two-storey design with the stable downstairs, many houses have three floors. Rock and wood are the body of the house, but most have glass windows and tin roofs.

The tin is less expensive and does not leak like the wooden shingles. Tourists complain that the tin roofs are ugly, until it starts to rain.

The shops all along this main street of Lukla are all closed behind wooden doors. Signs line the street — "South Col Garden Lodge," "Everest Air," "… for all your air-ticketing needs."

Cell phones are now an essential tool for planning cultural events.

In the twenty years I have known Lukla, the settlement has grown in size tenfold. The average size of buildings has quadrupled. Almost every building on the main street is a hotel for trekkers or a simple hostel for porters.

The rain pelts down harder, but Ang Maya is determined to continue. We turn off the main trail and follow a small track down the gentle slope that made this bench of land so attractive for an airstrip thirty years ago. Ang Maya carries an umbrella in one hand and a large Thermos full of tea in the other.

The village gonda is newly renovated with a cement courtyard and fresh prayer flags flutter on the tall poles. A newly built shelter lines one side of the courtyard, with a kitchen at the far end. At this full-moon time of the fourth Tibetan month, it is the annual Nyungne prayers to the god of compassion. Forty men, women and children either hurry about cooking or oversee the proceedings.

Lukla also now celebrates its own Dumchi festival. Most Sherpas here have come from other villages such as Thame, Nauche or Solu. Their sense of community is strong and someone has taken the leadership to start this tradition in the new village.

When I arrive in Nauche, dozens of people are up every morning to commemorate *Saka Dawa*, the special month of the Buddha. The monks spend weeks reading the religious books and doing

2010: Dumchi festival continues with the enthusiastic participation of young and old, except that in Nauche, the ritual to the protector deity is on the now forested slope.

pujas in various households, but in the spirit of Mahayana Buddhism, the benefit incurred spreads to the entire community, the world and all beings.

There are layers and layers beneath the tourist town façade.

In 1991 three brothers in Nauche sponsored a new observation of the *Nyungne* rites in the sixth month, which is usually August, when they would be home from trekking. Someone has sponsored the rites every year since.

Contrary to the assumption that tourism has robbed the Sherpas of their culture, it appears that the money tourism has brought to the community might be helping to proliferate cultural events.

Lhakpa counts a pile of money in her kitchen. She smiles and declares, "We've raised more money for Nyungne this year than in the past three years combined. But it's such a busy time of year; it's hard to expect too many people to come."

The main Sherpa villages all now have electricity.

A week later, it is not just the old people. There are a number of people in their thirties and forties, including one man who has climbed Everest several times and spends a lot of time in Kathmandu between expeditions. The kitchen is full of women who brought offerings of tea or helped to cook meals for the first day before the fasting begins.

It takes the leadership of a few individuals to make things happen, but it also takes the eagerness of the community to participate. Again the next year, the Sherpas in Nauche conduct Nyungne in both April and August.

I remember sitting around the hearth in the small kitchen of the "Sherpa Hotel" in Nauche in 1980. Everyone slept in one large room. The menu was potatoes, rice, more potatoes. Now three bakeries offer pastries and cappuccino.

The completion of the Thame electricity project has brought hydro power that is more reliable than Kathmandu's. Refrigerators and TV satellite dishes are in many middle-class and wealthier homes. Older women use a blender to mix butter tea and an electric hot plate to cook the stew for lunch.

Where once someone had to run to the national park headquarters with a radio request for a rescue, now tourists phone their families and friends anywhere in the world just to talk.

There are still the people for whom life is a day-to-day struggle. Certain families cultivated the connections that brought endless opportunities for education, loans, travel and prosperity.

Others struggle with the inflation created by the growing demand for food brought by the increase from 5,000 tourists per year in 1980 to over 20,000 twenty years later.

Potatoes are still dug by hand, and the traditional rules still regulate the annual herding of yaks. In places, the national park plantations have transformed bare hillsides into small forests.

More and more Sherpas have travelled, worked, lived or studied in Western countries. While most Sherpas still earn a living working with tourists on treks or in hotels, many now make a living in a variety of professions.

Sherpa friends were often the family members who made the transition from village life to modern occupations, such as tourism and conservation. Many have never returned to live in the Khumbu and several have stayed overseas when they completed their educations there. Some of their children have never lived in Khumbu, even though their families retain a strong Sherpa identity while living in Kathmandu.

Suddenly, they are realizing "we are the bridge" to maintain their culture.

Return to the Beyul

2008. In the late-afternoon mist, I hurry to arrive before dusk.

It has been almost three decades since my first arrival in the Khumbu beyul, the sanctuary of the Sherpas. The Khumbu has become a refuge, physically and spiritually.

The decades have been full of moments of exhilaration and dismay, joy and tragedy, realization and query. Always, I feel that I have learned something new every day.

Stepping carefully on the wet rocks, I pause as my cell phone rings.

"Didi [older sister], I need your advice. I have been offered a few months' work for the UN — in Chad. They have given me only today to decide," says Mingma.

I am surprised but not astounded, wondering what advice I could offer about this opportunity for a Sherpa to go work in Africa with a UN peacekeeping mission.

Mingma's father has worked many years in the trekking industry. He and Mingma's mother saved this money, took loans and gradually established a popular lodge in Nauche.

They sent Mingma to school in Kathmandu, where he excelled and got a scholarship to attend university in the United States. Upon graduation, Mingma returned to Nepal and found that despite dire "predictions" due to the insurgency in most parts of Nepal, he got a good job with the UN in Kathmandu.

Mingma was married with all the traditional rituals. Despite an overseas education, a technological job and a wife with a professional career, he keeps that inner culture of the Sherpas mentioned so often by Tengboche Rinpoche.

Not that modern influence necessarily precludes Sherpa culture. A strong sense of being Sherpa remains even among young people straddling the culture of their elders and the gadgets of the modern world. Cell phones facilitate making festival arrangements, and young Sherpas share news through websites.

Khumbila the mountain, from Tengboche

My first seven years in Nepal, in Khumbu, was an experience of the sacred. I met lamas, went on pilgrimage and was filled with the wonder of exploring a new culture and starting to see the world differently. I enriched my life, even though it set me off on a rather unusual "career path."

In 1995 I took work with a project to establish a national park in the Makalu-Barun area, east of Everest. This work used all my skills with conservation, communications and cultural subjects entwined with the natural environment.

This work helped me to start seeing beyond the beyul.

It offered the opportunity to spend time in neighbouring valleys to the south of Khumbu and with their Rai inhabitants, many of whom worked in hotels and homes of the Sherpas. In a village perched in the middle of a steep slope ten difficult days' walk from Khumbu, a village elder told me that 25 people from 16 households were working there. "Without Namche, we could not survive."

Work for development projects in more recent years has offered opportunities to talk to so many people in difficult circumstances — former bonded labourers, "untouchables," Hindu widows, and farmers without enough fields to feed their families. I came to realize how the systems of hierarchy went beyond discrimination to keep some people poor.

Where a century ago the Sherpas would migrate to find work in Darjeeling and British India, Khumbu has become an economic sanctuary for people from districts to the south and east. Those who do not find jobs still earn much-needed cash by bringing heavy loads of rice, millet, corn and wheat to sell at the weekly market. Others earn day wages carrying loads for merchants, trekking groups and local Sherpas.

As the profanity of conflict grew over Nepal's countryside, more and more young people would come to Khumbu from other districts to both make a living and escape. Many of us started to pay more attention to the inequities and poverty at the roots of the conflict. The conflict raised questions about our own prejudices and fears.

A tranquil stream on the way to Thame

Prayers in stone and on flags

The mudra, or hand gesture, of offering

Khumbu was less affected than most other places and trekking routes, which many Sherpas attributed to its history as a beyul. In 2003 I asked a Sherpa why he was building a large new hotel, despite the fact that fewer trekkers were coming to Nepal due to fear of the conflict. He replied with utter confidence, "Khumbu is a beyul; it will work out to be all right in the end."

"Hillary and so many foreigners have done so much for us Sherpas," says Tengboche Rinpoche, "so we cannot afford to ignore the problems of those who have not been so fortunate as to have Everest in their valley."

Just as working with the Sherpas opened my eyes to another way of perceiving the world, the conversations with these people helped me to understand the more difficult side of Nepal. They helped me to see both the sacred and the profane and start to understand and question world events in this era of intense politics and crisis.

Ultimately, we can build bridges of understanding between cultures in the world if we are not afraid just because they are different.

The Sherpas are just centred enough in their own values to be friendly with those who are different. They are confident enough to be tolerant. Perhaps intolerance comes from a lack of confidence.

Sherpas were open to this stranger, who became a friend. They shared their lives with me and did not flaunt the secrets that I could not know. Nor did I push to know them, either.

The Sherpas taught me that the world does not operate by right and wrong, in shades of black and white. There are many shades of grey, ways of perceiving problems and ways of finding our own solutions, which we already know deep inside us. The answers are within.

As Tengboche Rinpoche keeps reminding us, "The real beyul is our state of mind."

GLOSSARY

Abbot: One who can transmit monastic vows. Also a person who has attained a high degree of knowledge of dharma and is authorized to teach.

Ani: A Buddhist nun.

Beyul: A sacred place originally set aside by Guru Rinpoche as sanctuary from the troubled world.

Buddha: The Fully Awakened One, a being endowed with all enlightened qualities of realization. The historical Buddha lived over 2,500 years ago.

Chaam: Religious dance.

Chyenrezig: The bodhisattva (deity) personifying compassion of the Buddhas. Also called **Avalokiteshvara** in Sanskrit (Skt.).

Chorten (Tib.) (Skt.: **Stupa**): A monument symbolizing the Buddha's enlightenment.

Deity (Tib.: **Lha**; Skt.: **Deva**): A Buddha or wisdom deity, sometimes a dharma protector (such as Khumbila). May also refer to the personifications of enlightenment (such as Phawa Chyenrezig).

Enlightenment: The state of purification of all obscuration and the realization of all qualities, such as wisdom and compassion.

Gonda (Nepali: **Gompa**): Temple in village or monastery.

Guru Rinpoche: Established Buddhism in Tibet over 1,250 years ago, also **Padma Sambhava**.

Jomo Miyo Lungsangma: Female deity residing on Mt. Everest. Also called **Jomolungma** and **Chomolungma**.

Khata: A white or yellow scarf offered as a sign of respect or good wishes.

Khumbila: Protective deity of Khumbu. Also called **Khumbu-Yul-Lha** (Khumbu country-deity).

Lama (Skt.: **Guru**): A spiritual teacher and guide. A lama need not be a monk (thawa), and only a few monks are lamas. The word is sometimes used as a polite way to address a monk.

Lha: God, deity.

Lhakhang: "God's house": main room of a temple or an altar.

Lhapsang: Prayers by Sherpas to specified deity.

Mahadeva: A protector representing the action form of **Chyenrezig**, "great god."

Mahakala: A wrathful protector deity of Buddhism.

Mahayana: The tradition of Buddhism practised in China, Japan, Korea, Mongolia, Tibet and the Himalayan region. It aims to attain enlightenment for all beings and promote universal compassion to deliver all beings from suffering and its causes. The **Vajrayana** is a branch of the Mahayana.

Mandala (Skt.) (Tib.: **kyil khor**): A spiritual diagram with which the circular space of an enlightened being at the centre is visualized during Buddhist practices.

Mantra: Syllables recited to protect the mind of the practitioner from delusion and invoke the particular deity in the form of sound.

Merit: Positive energy arising from wholesome action or virtue.

Mudra: A ritual gesture performed with the hands.

Nangpa La: The pass between Khumbu and Tibet.

Ngagpa: Lay lama, minister.

Nyingmapa: The original sect of Tibetan Buddhism, also called the "Old Translation School." The followers of the first teachings translated and taught in Tibet.

Phachhen: First Sherpa to come to Khumbu.

Phardo: An intermediary state between death and subsequent rebirth.

Rinpoche: Title for high lamas and reincarnates.

Rongbuk: Monastery on north side of Everest.

Ru: Sherpa clans based on father's lineage; means "bones."

Sanskrit: Ancient language of India. Many words are Sanskrit (abbreviated Skt.).

Sherpa: Literally, sher-pa means "east-people."

Stupa (Skt.) (Tib.: **Chorten**): A monument symbolizing the Buddha's enlightenment. Stupas are the most typical Buddhist monuments and are found in a variety of forms. They often contain the relics of enlightened beings or lamas.

Thawa: Monk.

Torma: A ritual object, often modelled from tsampa and butter, which can symbolize a deity, mandala or offering, or a weapon to fight negative forces.

Tsampa: Flour made from roasted barley or other grains. A staple food in the Himalaya.

Whang: Blessing ceremony.

Wisdom: The ability to correctly understand emptiness and the nature of the mind.

The Khumbu Valley

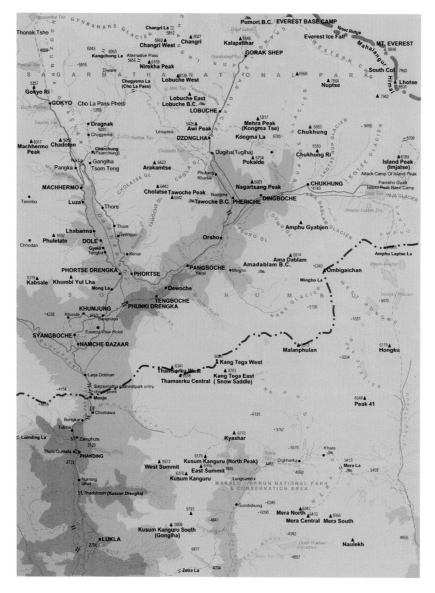

SELECTED READING

Bernbaum, Edwin. *The Way to Shambhala: A Search for the Mythical Kingdom beyond the Himalayas*. Garden City, N.Y.: Anchor Press/ Doubleday, 1980.

Brower, Barbara. *Sherpa of Khumbu: People, Livestock and Landscape*. Delhi: Oxford University Press, 1991.

Downs, Hugh R. *Rhythms of a Himalayan Village*. San Francisco: Harper & Row Publishers, 1980.

Fisher, James K. *Sherpas: Reflections on Change in Himalayan Nepal*. Berkeley: University of California Press, 1990.

Fürer-Haimendorf, Christoph von. *The Sherpas of Nepal: Buddhist Highlanders*. Berkeley: University of California Press, 1964.

Gold, Peter. *Tibetan Reflections: Life in a Tibetan Refugee Community*. London: Wisdom Publications, 1984.

Norbu, Thubten Jigme, and Colin Turnbull. *Tibet: Its History, Religion and People*. London: Penguin Books, 1968.

Ortner, Sherry B. *Sherpas through their Rituals*. Cambridge: Cambridge University Press, 1978.

Ortner, Sherry B. *Life and Death on Mt. Everest: Sherpas and Himalayan Mountaineering*. Princeton: Princeton University Press, 1999.

Sherpa, Lhakpa Norbu. *Through a Sherpa Window: Illustrated Guide to Traditional Sherpa Culture*. Kathmandu: Vajra Publications, 2008.

Stevens, Stanley F. *Claiming the High Ground: Sherpas, Subsistence and Environmental Change in the Highest Himalaya*. Berkeley: University of California Press, 1993.

Wangmo, Jamyang. *Lawudo Lama: Stories of Reincarnation from the Mount Everest Region*. Kathmandu: Vajra Publications, 2005.

Zangbu, Ngawang Tenzin (Abbot of Tengboche Monastery). *Stories and Customs of the Sherpas*. Edited by Frances Klatzel. Kathmandu: Mera Publications, 2000.